GENDER AND PASTORAL CARE:

The personal-social aspects of the whole school

Blackwell Studies in Personal and Social Education and Pastoral Care

Edited by Peter Lang and Peter Ribbins

Leading a Pastoral Team
Les Bell and Peter Maher

Supportive Education
Phil Bell and Ron Best

School Discipline
Chris Watkins and Patsy Wagner

The Pastoral Curriculum
Lesley Bulman and David Jenkins

The Evaluation of Pastoral Care
Tony Clemett and John Pearce

Special Needs in Ordinary Classrooms
Gerda Hanko

Assessing and Recording Achievement
Stephen Munby

The Form Tutor
Philip Griffiths and Keith Sherman

GENDER AND PASTORAL CARE:

The personal-social aspects of the whole school

Edited by
Colleen McLaughlin
Caroline Lodge
Chris Watkins

First published 1991

Published by
Basil Blackwell Ltd
108 Cowley Road
Oxford OX4 1JF
England

British Library Cataloguing in Publication Data
McLaughlin, Colleen
  Gender and pastoral care.
  1. Secondary schools. Students. Sex roles. Development
  I. Title
  370.19345

  ISBN 0–631–17176–2
  ISBN 0–631–17177–0 pbk

Typeset in 10/12pt Plantin
by Graphicraft Typesetters Ltd, Hong Kong
Printed in Great Britain
by T.J. Press (Padstow) Limited.

Contents

SECTION THREE: WORKING WITH INDIVIDUALS AND FAMILIES: THE GENDER ELEMENTS

Preface

Most teachers recognise the significance of gender as an important educational issue. Indeed, the National Curriculum Council has identified equal opportunities as one of the major cross-curricular dimensions. Many of those involved in pastoral care would almost certainly claim that it has a major role to play in addressing the gender-related problems that research has shown exist in many schools and in the practice of a number of teachers. The need to eradicate sexism and provide genuine equal opportunities cannot easily be separated from a school's overall responsibility for the personal and social development of its pupils. However, although over recent years the level of awareness has heightened considerably, something reflected in the number of policy statements and guidelines emerging at LEA and school level, the actual impact on practice has been limited. A possible reason for this has been that specific guidance on what should actually be done has not always been readily available. In the case of pastoral care and personal and social education this has certainly been so; some of the most widely used programmes offer very little work in relation to gender.

It is clear that pastoral care and personal and social education can play a major role in coordinating and delivering a school's policy and practice in terms of gender. This book provides one of the first attempts to draw out the implications of this and provide a coherent and manageable approach which has potential for operating at a number of levels. In fact the contribution that the writers make goes beyond the specifics of pastoral care and offers stimulus, insight and ideas to anyone with a concern for gender-related issues in school.

What the writers have presented is a clear and very practical approach to a difficult area of policy and practice. In doing this they have broken a considerable amount of new ground; the book includes much that is new both in terms of analysis and theory and also in terms of specific suggestions for practice. This book's value is increased through its potential as a source book for specific ideas and insights and its provision of a coherent, logical and practical overall approach.

Peter Lang
Peter Ribbins
Series editors

Introduction

Much has been written about schools and gender, in both a broad and a highly specific fashion. This book focuses on gender, pastoral care, personal and social development, areas which have not been drawn together explicitly before. We have in mind a reader who is not steeped in the literature and research on gender and schools, but who may be coming to this area for the first time, and who may be coming to this book because of a desire to interweave the strands of gender, pastoral care and personal and social development.

Pastoral care and personal/social education

By pastoral care is meant those aspects of schooling which focus on young people's needs for welfare, guidance, order and their learning about themselves and others. This definition will be developed further later. Pastoral care can become trivialised and distorted in many ways. It can become trivialised by being split and separated from the academic aspects of the school, even from the area of personal and social education in the curriculum. It can become distorted if pastoral care systems are turned into reactive punishment systems. In this book we view pastoral care and personal/social education as inextricably linked; as a dimension of the whole school; and as a dimension of every teacher's work.

To examine further what is meant by pastoral care I will use the framework adopted for this book. The various facets of pastoral work have been divided into three areas:[1]

1

pastoral casework
pastoral aspects of the curriculum
pastoral management.

By *pastoral casework* is meant those aspects of our work which focus on an individual pupil and her or his development. This will involve viewing the pupil in the context of her or his family and culture. In this area teachers may be involved in a variety of activities. They may be reviewing progress, guiding pupils through choices, counselling pupils over learning or personal issues or dealing with home/school links. The teacher may be mediator, advocate, counsellor or change agent.

By *pastoral aspects of the curriculum* is meant a focus on pupils and their personal, social, and moral learnings in the school setting. This is an area which requires planning and monitoring and which encompasses all aspects of the school's curriculum. There is a need to look at whole-school processes and adopt an integrative approach, rather than trying to reduce this demanding task to running a PSE course or cramming everything into a 20 minute tutorial session. This area requires a clarification of the distinctive contributions of *all* locations, such as subject lessons, PSE courses, tutorial programmes and other locations.

> And it will need to be based on a whole-person view of the pupils in our schools, a view which recognises young people's developments in bodily self, social self, sexual self, vocational self, and moral/political self.[2]

As the National Curriculum Council Guidance 3 *The Whole Curriculum* [1990] reminds us,

> The successful management of the whole depends upon a corporate plan for the whole school, embracing all aspects of the whole curriculum... It lies in securing equality of access and opportunity for each pupil. It lies in the best use of existing and planned resources based on audits of the existing curriculum, resources, buildings, staff and equipment. It lies in decisions about regular procedures through which the business of the school is conducted towards the pupil and his or her work, towards the school community as a whole, and towards those outside the school...[3]

The development of whole school policies leads us into the third area of pastoral work – *pastoral management*. This area of work focuses on the school, its climate or ethos, its management of staff, its relation to parents and others, and how effective it is in reaching its goals. Here an overview can be taken and the task is one of managing the entitlement of every pupil to guidance, welfare and access to a planned learning experience.

Pastoral care/PSE and gender

There has been much research which clearly shows that schools have an impact on the gender beliefs and behaviours of their pupils. Similarly, we know that the learning experiences of pupils are often differentiated on the basis of gender. This has led to an acknowledgement by bodies such as the National Curriculum Council that the school curriculum needs to take account of the promotion of equality of opportunity for all pupils, regardless of ethnic origin and gender [NCC 1990]. Equal opportunities is described by the NCC as a cross-curricular dimension.

> Dimensions such as a commitment to providing equal opportunities for all pupils, and a recognition that preparation for life in a multicultural society is relevant to all pupils, should permeate every aspect of the curriculum.[4]

The advice to schools by the NCC is more fully discussed by Chris Watkins in his introduction to Section 2 of this book.

Pastoral care, as previously defined, has a major contribution to make to equal opportunities work. In dealings with individual pupils, in the curriculum and in the management of these, teachers are impacting on gender beliefs and behaviours. This needs to be work that is scrutinised and planned, rather than ad hoc. Any view of a school's contribution to and management of an entitlement to equality which took no account of the pastoral contribution would be partial and remiss. In addition to the scrutiny of existing practice, the facets of pastoral work will form a large element of the school's planned contribution to the principle of equality of access and opportunity.

The structure of the book

The contribution of pastoral care and its connection with gender is the substance of this work. The function of the book is to examine and debate the three major areas earlier defined as aspects of pastoral work.

Chapter 1 addresses some of the issues in working with gender in schools. It focuses particularly on different stances which we can take to working with teachers in this complex field. The first section which follows is entitled *The Institutional Context*. In it, the three contributors address the wide setting of the school and the LEA. Caroline Lodge explores the complex workings of the school as an institution in its interplay with gender and pastoral care. Lesley Kant explores the role of the LEA and finally, Jennifer Walden explores gender in the classroom.

The second section explores the pastoral aspects of the curriculum. Chris Watkins, in his introduction and chapter, examines what we mean by pastoral aspects of the curriculum, how they interrelate to gender work, and why this is a necessary task. Gill Venn highlights the issues for teachers and pupils when working with the complex processes associated with gender beliefs and behaviours. Sue Askew and Carol Ross discuss the response a school might take to a planned learning offer and argue for an integrative approach.

The final section addresses the pastoral casework facets. Colleen McLaughlin explores the issues and processes of working with individual pupils. Patsy Wagner explores the gender issues in working with and communicating with families. Fuller summaries of section contents can be found in the introduction to each section.

The book aims to have coherence and development but, at the same time, we acknowledge that the reader may choose to read selectively according to their needs. It is hoped that the book can be used in both ways and that it will make a useful contribution to our exploration of working more effectively with gender issues in the field of pastoral care in schools.

References

1 Watkins, C. [1985] 'Does Pastoral Care = Personal and Social Education?' *Pastoral Care in Education*. Vol 3, No 3. November, 1985.
2 Watkins, C. [1990] 'The Pastoral Agenda at Easter 1990' *Pastoral Care in Education*. Vol 8, No 4, 3–9.
3 NCC [1990] *The Whole Curriculum* National Curriculum Council, York, p 7.
4 *Ibid*, p 2.

1
Looking at gender

Colleen McLaughlin

Wearing a certain set of spectacles

On Saturday I stood in the queue for the check-out in my local super-
market. In front of me were two families with their respective children.
The first trolley was surrounded by mother, father and three girls. The
second trolley was surrounded by mother and father and two boys. I
watched with fascination. The older girl pushed the trolley to the 'load'
position, marshalled her two younger sisters into a safe place and proceeded
to silently unpack and load. When this was over she stood aside and said to
her sisters, 'Hold my hand and we'll go outside now'.

The trolley of family number two approached the check-out. The two
boys, who were of similar age to the girl, sat in the basket of the trolley and
loudly shot each other with imaginary guns, oblivious to the people and
tasks being undertaken around them. I was aware that one possible view is
that this is a micro-picture of the difference in expectation, role and behaviour between boys and girls. I was also struck by the fact that I am so
aware of these little scenes. I have in the last ten years acquired a set of
spectacles which show up gender difference and sex-stereotyping: I now see
the world through these spectacles. Acquiring them has not been comfortable, nor has it always been a straightforward process – this I will return to
later.

What happens if we look at schools through these spectacles? Clearly,
there is a similar picture of difference in role, behaviour and expectation.
The source of gender difference and the role of schools in the creation of
gender identity is not yet clear and will not be explored in depth here.
However, a review of the evidence tells us that schools not only acknowledge and operate on these differences but that they 'amplify' them. The
growing body of evidence depicts classrooms organised on the basis of sex;
girls and boys receiving differentiated treatment within the classroom; and

girls and boys interpreting their success and failure in different ways. Dweck and Licht show girls perceiving their failure as personal and their successes as a matter of chance. We have evidence that,

> in primary schools girls do better on average in most standard-ised tests of attainment. At the secondary school girls do better in school leaving examinations. In both GCE 'O' levels and CSE exams they obtain higher grades than their male peers.[2]

Yet girls do not choose to enter fully into certain areas of the curriculum, such as the physical sciences and technology, and they have low aspirations. This rather simplistic selection from some of the evidence shows that there is cause for concern: the experience of schooling and classrooms is heavily dependent on sex, young people have a sense of their worth reinforced or adapted on the basis of gender, and they leave schools with different aspirations and opportunities, also related to gender.

What if we turn to look at the staff of the school with that same set of spectacles? Here too we can see that sex and gender make a difference. There are big discrepancies in terms of the positions held and a whole mythology exists about the reasons for this. Women are seriously under-represented in senior positions and myths such as 'women do not want promotion' or 'women teachers are less qualified than their male colleagues' still abound.[3]

It is possible, then, to view schools through a certain set of spectacles and see inequality in terms of power for women teachers, and to see persons ostensibly not valued in the same way. It is possible to read of boys describing girls as 'invisible', to read of teachers expecting girls to fit into certain predictable jobs despite their desire not to, or their ability to perform at a much different level. There is plenty of 'objective' evidence to use to prove the point, should we wish to do so. At times, I felt this was the only necessary task; I adopted the 'road to Damascus' approach, believing that if confronted with the facts and figures then people would change. I also felt that this was all that had to happen, after all, people are rational beings – they would soon realise the errors of their ways and see the world through my eyes. This has been described as the 'brute sanity' approach.

An example of this is when a colleague and I addressed a large group of secondary headteachers at the request of one of the LEA officers. We began by explaining to the group that there was a wealth of evidence to consider. We presented the facts and the statistics. We set up an exercise where the head teachers were asked to consider both the state of their school and the state of their attitudes. After three hours, I realised that these teachers still had not accepted the view we were putting forward and they clearly felt threatened. In the final session comments such as, 'But what would happen if women changed? Who would have the children?' or 'It's not so good at the top, you know,' were issuing forth. The lesson to be learnt here is that an 'objective' approach is too simplistic; it does not take into account the personal and complex nature of examining the area of gender in schooling. It is not enough simply to say 'This is the position and now we will get on with changing it'. The evidence had been there for a good decade now.

The nature of the task

The task is one of reflection and examination of our own learning: reflection about the position of young persons in schooling and the nature of the experience they receive related to their gender. Underpinning this process is a set of values. These are,

> that personal worth should be equally attributed to all young people, regardless of sex, race, class, religion, or any other division, and that this belief should be adopted by all schools. In this context we describe as 'sexism' those discriminatory practices, relationships, power relations, attitudes, and beliefs which uphold gender differences and attribute differential worth to a person on the basis of their sex. Sexism thus damages and dehumanises by encouraging people, both men and women, into partial views of their own and others' identity, society and history.[4]

Not everyone holds these as self-evident and, if they do, the process of achieving this state of affairs is seen very differently according to our own experiences and learnings about gender. It is very important to start from this acknowledgement of difference.

If schools, teachers, and pupils are to reflect upon their positions then there are three main arenas for reflection – the individual, the classroom and the school. There are other areas of work such as that of the LEA and the community, but I shall focus on the immediate school context here.

Individual reflection

Working in the area of gender is a personal process. It is about views of ourselves, feelings about power and relationships between the sexes and notions of worth. Teachers hold different views and are at different points. We know that these attitudes are related to many things, for example, subject specialism is one factor. Talking about gender is often perceived as controversial and political; it can be personally threatening.

The idea that girls and boys are basically equal and should have the same opportunities in education seems to be well accepted by teachers. But the idea that there are informal barriers to equal opportunities or that the present system is biased towards boys, is still highly contentious.[5]

This is not grounds for despair, rather it is an argument for accepting that there are widely varying positions, dependent upon age, subject specialism, sex, personal experience, and even regional location.

If we are asking teachers to examine the way they 'see' then the affective aspect of teacher learning must be acknowledged. We must realise that 'professional development is also personal – and so, inevitably, emotional, untidy, difficult, risky and sometimes downright unpleasant.'[6] If individual reflection is to occur then the process should be characterised by a sense of purpose, a sense of control, a sense of support, a sense of self and a sense of success. Unless teacher reflection is characterised by these elements, little change will occur; teachers will find ways of minimising change or administrative developments if they are not committed. Unless individual reflections on attitudes to sex and gender equity happen in a climate of respect for difference and feeling, teachers will feel threatened and could harden their positions rather than open them up for examination.

It is helpful to remember some aspects of what we know about individual change and institutional development. All change is inevitably likely to cause anxiety and feel personal to teachers and pupils alike.[7] When working with individual teachers and groups certain skills have been identified as helpful.[8] Change will be aided by listening to others, respecting others' views and having some ability to work with and understand groups. A problem-solving approach is the most helpful one to adopt, since it means learning will then be seen as a central element. Passion, strong views and total commitment to an ideology can block the process of development and polarise positions and attitudes.

The previous discussion has focused on teachers, their attitudes and their reflections. Pupils will also be involved in this process of individual reflection and all the characteristics of the process will also apply to them. It is very important that pupils are included in this process.

Classroom reflection

As has been shown, the classroom is central to discussion and reflection on gender equity. However, the nature of classrooms and teacher-pupil interactions makes this work difficult to undertake for teachers on their own. Classrooms are busy places where teachers may be involved in up to one thousand interactions a day. It is difficult to monitor what is happening given the pace of classroom activity. Teachers plan what they are going to do beforehand and reflect on it afterwards; rarely can they afford the luxury of reflecting on events at the time of their occurrence. Dale Spender[9] reminds us also that we see what we wish to see. This is another strand in the complex web of classroom reflection. What we see will be constrained by the spectacles we have always worn. The process of classroom observation and self-assessment is then part of the process of individual reflection and is a very important part of the learning process for teachers.

Complexity is cause for thought, not reason for inaction. As teachers we have a lot of power.

> Teachers have the power to determine the reality in their classrooms and to 'block' the learning of their pupils; they are the authority figures and they can decree 'how it really is.'[10]

Teachers can change their practice if they are aware that they may be reinforcing potentially harmful stereotypes or harmful patterns of interaction, but it is often a long and complex process if it is undertaken individually, due to the busy nature of classrooms.

Luxton[11] has a useful framework for reflecting on the classroom, which he calls the four Cs – context, content, cognitive style and competence.

1 Context
Here we are examining the context of learning. Our classrooms are often organised on the basis of gender. Some questions that may be asked about classroom practice are: How are pupils seated in the classroom? Are pupils grouped according to sex and should they be allowed to have this choice? What are the results of this? How is teacher time allocated? Do certain groups receive more help? How is language used in the classroom? Does it have effects on pupils' perceptions of their worth and power? How do pupils themselves interact in the classroom? These questions help to examine the affective environment of the classroom.

2 Content
Here the focus is on the content of the learning and teaching on offer. It would include an examination of the materials used in the classroom with a view to reflecting on the gender images portrayed and the access pupils have to them. Are some materials more girl or boy-friendly?

3 Cognitive style
This cannot be separated from content as it is to do with the delivery of the content and the cognitive styles used. If we look at the take-up of subjects and the imbalance shown, if we also look at the work done on gender and cognitive style, then we must take note of the different ways in which boys and girls work. I am not saying that girls and boys are different in terms of their 'innate' abilities, but there is evidence that certain ways of thinking are

stereotyped. An example might be that the scientific way of thinking is portrayed as masculine, even if this is unjustified. What images are we giving? Are we using a range of teaching styles in the classroom so that all pupils are given access to the learning?

4 Competence

This area of examination is about achievements and gender images of competence. Abilities can be stereotyped, as can contexts and content. I would like to cite a personal example. I was once told that I drove like a man. It felt like and was intended as a compliment about my competence: it also felt like a slap in the face to my femininity. Monitoring is key here and there are some useful, comprehensive schedules in existence. Two are *Genderwatch*[12] and *Greater Expectations*.[13]

School reflection

In working towards gender equity in a school one of the key tasks is to discover the 'hidden messages' sent through the curriculum and the institution. This is a now familiar phrase but schools are not yet fully conversant with the task itself. It is to examine the whole workings from the perspective of gender. If a school is embarking on developing a positive approach to sex and gender equity then it is necessary to appraise the present values in operation and do 'a testing of the waters' in order to have some guide to the fit with the proposed development.

I have mentioned values, which are important, but there needs to be mention here also of power. There is a political dimension to gender reflection and development. Teachers need to be aware of this when reflecting on the position of their school. What is being asked here is that schools work towards the same degree of self-knowledge as teachers.

The community and its expectations needs to be mentioned briefly too. Reflecting on gender equity has been described here as involving individual, classroom and school reflection. There is another aspect and that is the expectations of the community in which the school is based. The values of the adults in the community are very important. Parents, like teachers, will hold different views on gender expectation and this will affect the work in school and the view of young people on the work done in school. Schools will need to take on the task of review and exploration with parents as well as teachers and pupils.

Another factor is the LEA. One of the things we know is that teachers often look to the LEA for support and a lead in this area of work. As has already been said, this work can be seen as controversial and, therefore, LEA support can be significant.

Conclusion

In many schools today the situation is one of inequality between the sexes, of worth being unequally distributed and of power imbalance. This is clearly of concern. Over the last decade there have been developments in terms of how this issue may be approached. If schools are to begin to work towards remedying this then attention must be paid to the processes used in that development. It is helpful to view the process as one of learning, to which we bring all the best of what we know about pupils' and teachers' learning. It is also a process which can occur at different levels – there is no need to wait for total consensus before reflection is undertaken. The individual teacher can do much to examine her/his own individual practice.

References

1   Dweck, C. and Licht, B. (1983) 'Sex differences in achievement orientations: consequences for academic choices and attainments.' in Marland, M. (ed.) (1983) *Sex Differentiation and Schooling*. Heinemann.
2   Blackstone, T. (1986) Introduction to *Girl-Friendly Schooling*. Whyte, J. et al. Methuen. p iii.
3   Davidson, H. (1986) 'Unfriendly myths about women teachers.' in Whyte, J. et al (1986) *Girl-Friendly Schooling*. Methuen.
4   NAPCE (1986) 'The pastoral contribution to sex and gender equity' National Association for Pastoral Care in Education.
5   Kelly, A. (1987) 'Traditionalists and trendies: teachers' attitudes to educational issues.' in Weiner, G. and Arnot, M. (1987) *Gender Under Scrutiny*. Open University.
6   Drummond, M-J. (1988) 'Learning about gender in primary schools.' in Lang, P. (ed.) (1988) *Thinking About...Personal and Social Education in the Primary School*. Blackwell.
7   Fullan, M. (1982) *The Meaning of Educational Change*. Teachers' College Press: Colombia University.
8   Schmuck, R. and Runkel, P. (1985) *The Handbook of Organization Development in Schools*. Third edition. Mayfield Publishing, London.
9   Spender, D. (1982) *Invisible Women: the Schooling Scandal*. Chameleon Books.
10 Spender, D. (1983) 'Telling how it is: language and gender in the classroom.' in Marland, M. (ed.) (1983) *Sex Differentiation and Schooling*. Heinemann.

11 Luxton, R. (1987) Unpublished talk.
12 Myers, K. (1987) *Genderwatch*. Schools Curriculum Development Council.
13 Szirom, T. and Dyson, S. (1986) *Greater Expectations*. Learning Development Aids.

Further reading

Chisholm, L. and Holland, J. (1987) 'Anti-sexist action research in school: the Girls and Occupational Choice Project.' in Weiner, G. and Arnot, M. (eds.) (1987) *Gender Under Scrutiny*. Open University.
Marland, M. (ed.) (1983) *Sex Differentiation and Schooling*. Heinemann.
Millman, V. (1984) 'Teacher as researcher: a new tradition for research on gender.' in Weiner, G. and Arnot, M. (eds.) (1987) *Gender Under Scrutiny*. Open University.
Pratt, J. et al (1986) 'The attitudes of teachers.' in Whyte, J. et al (eds.) (1986) *Girl-Friendly Schooling*. Methuen.
Randall, G. (1987) 'Gender differences in pupil-teacher interaction in workshops and laboratories.' in Weiner, G. and Arnot, M. (eds.) (1987) *Gender Under Scrutiny*. Open University.
Stanworth, M. (1983) 'Girls on the margins: a study of gender divisions in the classroom.' in Weiner, C. and Arnot, M. (eds.) (1987) *Gender Under Scrutiny*. Open University.
Weiner, G. and Arnot, M. (1988) *Gender and Education Bibliography – the Open University*, available from Kim Watts, The Open University, 527 Frichley Road, London NW3 7B9.

SECTION ONE
THE INSTITUTIONAL
CONTEXT

Introduction

Caroline Lodge

The three chapters in this section each look at the ways in which organisational and institutional processes and structures can help or hinder gender equity.

The systems and organisation of schools, LEAs and classrooms can advance or hinder gender equity. A phrase which has been used to describe this process is 'institutional sexism'. Institutional sexism is used to mean the processes in an organisation through which gender inequity is reinforced. This can happen, for example, by unconsciously accepting prevailing attitudes, by creating systems which might unintentionally prevent women or girls taking advantage of an opportunity, or by not providing opportunities for girls and women.

Each of the three chapters looks at the ways in which the processes used in institutions can be examined and then changed in order to promote gender equity. The section begins with an examination of the systems in a school as they are so powerful in helping or hindering gender equity. We then look at the wider institution of the LEA and follow that with a focus on the classroom. Each chapter argues that this approach succeeds best when it is consistent. For example: encouraging pupils to examine stereotyping through the curriculum, or promoting positive images of women will have a limited effect if the structure of the school or LEA, or experience in that school or LEA, give a contradictory message.

Each chapter also reinforces a central theme of this book: that the best results will be gained through the development of explicit policy, developed by all staff and understood and carried through by all members of the service. It is argued that essential parts of policy implementation are the processes of review and monitoring.

It is also clear that the development and implementation of such policies will produce reactions, as all change does. Much of this reaction will be negative and frustrating. Those leading the process must use the skills and qualities associated with sensitivity and determination. An understanding of how change can be brought about must be combined with realistic setting of targets and an ability to recognise and acclaim progress.

The most effective change will be achieved through wide discussion and a feeling of shared ownership of the purpose and methods. But the individual is also able to influence the experiences of the pupils. This is the second theme of each chapter. This can be achieved, for example, by asking the right questions of the right people, by using an explicit rationale for classroom organisation, and by helping change the policy of the LEA.

What is clear is that when schools, LEAs and individual teachers ignore how the organisation of pastoral care affects gender equity they will be helping to perpetuate gender inequity.

2

Gender, pastoral care and the whole school: policy and action

Caroline Lodge

Introduction

An institution which has a clear idea of what 'pastoral' means, and which has thought through how gender issues are to be dealt with in all aspects of school life will be an institution which is dealing fairly with its students. Few schools have a clear pastoral policy, and although many have equal opportunities policies, few have worked out how they should be implemented. These two aspects of school life remain divorced, rather than reinforcing each other. This chapter examines how pastoral structures and the school as an institution can operate to discourage or support gender equity and how those working within schools and institutions can begin to examine and affect some of this.

Why is it important to consider pastoral care alongside gender issues? It is useful to consider what it is that these two facets of school life have in common. A useful way of considering the broad aim of pastoral care is given by Watkins: '...the specific contribution of pastoral care is to bring attention to the personal and interpersonal dimensions, and to give a pupil-centred focus'.[1] Here there is a very clear link with gender issues, for it is in the personal and interpersonal aspects of school life that gender issues are experienced. Equal opportunities policies address the experiences of pupils at school *as girls* or *as boys*. Young people build up their image of themselves, their gender identity, through the relationships and interactions they experience with other people.

In every area of pastoral care in secondary school there is a gender aspect which should be considered: in pastoral casework, in pastoral curriculum and in pastoral management which is the theme of this chapter. Most secondary schools have a pastoral system, that is, a structure for the delivery of pastoral care. The structure, whether it is in houses or years, is only a mechanism for delivery of pastoral care. It is the understanding of the teaching staff, and the experience of the parents and pupils, which will determine whether pastoral care is delivered in a way which promotes gender equity.

The way in which a school organises its pastoral care affects attitudes and behaviour, including attitudes and practice in gender-related areas. For example: does the school offer positive role models or is it reinforcing stereotypical roles in its pastoral structure? Does it have a consistent policy of opposing offensive comments (including sexist remarks) or does it allow its members to respond individually? In short, do the structures of the school and the pastoral care offered by the school support the equal opportunities aims and objectives of the school?

This chapter argues the need for three inter-related and overlapping stages:

1 Identification of and research into sexist processes in the school's pastoral organisation;
2 Work on changing those processes;
3 Building change, review and evaluation into the system.

At a time when the educational context in which schools operate is changing rapidly and radically, it is important that issues to do with pastoral care and gender are not lost. For example: schools have had to create a new structure for allocation of posts of responsibility with the imposition of incentive allowances to replace the Burnham points system. It is possible that both equal opportunities and pastoral posts may be lost in new structures as schools try to reinforce curriculum (and especially National Curriculum) weighting. It may not follow that schools with fewer or lower status pastoral posts than formerly will have a weaker or less effective pastoral system, but the dangers are apparent.

It is also important to look at the limitations to change imposed by external influences upon an institution: these may be political, cultural or economic. However, those working in the field of gender should also take strength from alliances with anti-racists and anti-heterosexists. Some of our battles run alongside. While we struggle to maintain good practice we can draw strength from remembering that good educational practice is anti-sexist.

Identifying sexist processes in the school's pastoral organisation

The staff of a school need a shared understanding of the purpose and workings of a pastoral system, as well as a shared understanding of gender inequities and how they can be tackled effectively. In many schools individual staff view the pastoral system very differently. They could be placed along a continuum: at one end would be those teachers for whom 'pastoral' is used as a more acceptable word for 'control'. At the other end would be those who believe that the personal and social development of each pupil is the concern of the school.

Similarly there are many schools where the staff range from those who feel that equal opportunities or gender issues are irrelevant to school life to those who feel they are the concern of everyone. Until there is open discussion of information, different viewpoints and ideas on both pastoral and gender issues, there will be no progress toward a shared broad view, and the pupils will receive confused messages.

I know of few schools which have developed a pastoral policy. I have experience of several schools where the definition of pastoral was not shared, or even much explored, by the whole staff. This is partly because pastoral care is elusive as a precise concept. The goals of a pastoral system have been usefully described as including the following:

- to provide a point of continuing personal contact for every pupil;
- to offer support and guidance on issues affecting pupils' development and achievement;
- to promote the development of curriculum, organisation and pedagogy to meet the personal-social and vocational needs of pupils;
- to monitor individual progress and achievement;
- to use external agencies to meet pupils' needs;
- to develop a structure to enable these goals to be realised and evaluated.[2]

The structure which any school develops to meet all or some of these goals must also be designed, monitored and reviewed with gender considerations very much to the fore. Some examples quickly show how important this is. The point of continuing personal contact is usually a tutor. The tutor is important in many pupils' lives and therefore it is essential that the tutor's own attitudes are as free of assumptions and prejudices about girls and boys as possible. The guidance and support offered to pupils must not be based on assumptions that girls and boys have different destinies. The development of the curriculum must take into account the differing experiences of girls and boys, but not accept differing levels of achievement based on a pupil's sex. Development of these points is the substance of this book, but in this chapter I shall focus on examining the pastoral structure and ethos of a school from this gender perspective.

The most effective examination of any links between pastoral policy and a gender perspective should involve discussion with teachers, parents, governors and the pupils themselves. All these groups should be involved in defining terms and deciding upon aims, objectives and implementation. Only in this way will all who have a part to play in the school feel they own the process of change.

There are five broad areas which would benefit from the attention suggested:

1 Staff issues
2 Physical resources
3 Environmental issues
4 Administration
5 Hidden curriculum

1 Staff issues

Recruitment and status

The relative position of men and women in schools is often a very potent symbol for the pupils and other members of staff. Most school staffing structures contain a majority of women receiving the lower allowances. This was certainly the general pattern of the Burnham structure, and may have been further emphasised by the imposition of the new incentive allowances, which has reinforced hierarchy in schools and caused pastoral structures to shrink. The HMI survey of Pastoral Care in Schools[3] revealed that men held most of the posts of responsibility in the pastoral structures in the schools on which they were reporting.

While recruitment and allocation of incentive allowances is a matter primarily for headteachers and governors there are some useful questions which can be asked about the allocation of pastoral responsibilities and about encouraging women to apply for more senior posts [see page 27]. Those with responsibilities for interviewing, especially governors, would benefit from training which enabled them to encourage both women and men to show themselves to their best advantage.

Roles, role models and expectations

Many women teachers would agree that a common assumption among colleagues and pupils is that women are 'softer' than men, that men maintain better discipline than women or are 'harder'. This attitude can make it difficult for women, especially when it is grafted on to notions about what pastoral post-holders should be doing anyway. In a school where the head of year/house is expected to maintain the discipline of the school, to be the person to whom 'problem' children are referred and the person who is supposed to 'do something' about certain pupils, a woman can experience great difficulty.

A recent study of 24 comprehensive schools threw up the finding that women post-holders often have dual roles, sometimes at a lower grade. They often hold 'complex, cross-school jobs' which are particular to their institution. The report suggested that women's cross-school skills were often being ignored and omitted from senior management level, where they would be invaluable.[4]

It would be worth examining the job specifications of pastoral postholders and tutors to consider what the overt expectations of the school are. This would raise wider questions about the conceptions of pastoral care, discipline, and so forth within the school; it could also raise questions about the way in which a postholder or tutor is expected to carry out their duties. It would then be worth extending the examination to look at roles in action, to see where principle and practice match or do not fit.

Training and staff development for pastoral care

Considerations about role and task lead naturally into considerations about training for this aspect of a teacher's work. It is well documented that initial training generally gives scant attention to pastoral aspects of teaching.[5] The same could be said for training on gender-related issues. The scheme to introduce untrained (licensed) teachers directly into the classroom will also need to be closely watched to ensure that trainees see their role as wider than merely teaching their subject. Training will need to include aspects of pastoral care. There is a need for each team and each individual to look at professional practice and development in the light of current thinking on pastoral care and gender.

It is axiomatic that the social and personal aspects of education enter into all areas of school life, and do not affect just what happens during registration time, or tutorial time. The National Curriculum Council has acknowledged this:

> Personal and social development involves aspects of teaching and learning which should permeate all of the curriculum... It is the responsibility of all teachers and is equally important in all phases of education.[6]

The term 'Pastoral Curriculum' has been used by Marland to describe the planned teaching of matters to do with personal and social development, wherever they occur in the curriculum.[7] The term 'hidden curriculum' was used to describe all the unplanned interaction which takes place within a school. Both aspects of school life need to be included in the training of all teachers, and not merely at the initial stage.

2 Physical resources

There are clear messages in the way schools deploy their physical resources. These reflect the differentiation in value between sectors of the school. A simple example is the use of office accommodation, and who gets it. In one school heads of year who wanted to have private interviews with pupils or parents had to beg the use of a private space from those who had been allocated office accommodation. Clearly their work was less valued than that of the fortunate few who had the status and convenience of an office. For pupils and pastoral care there are some important, everyday issues to explore.

Space in general is an interesting and under-researched aspect of school life, especially the use of free space – corridors and playgrounds. Observation of the interaction of the users of these areas will give interesting information about the school. Do pupils give way to teachers on crowded corridors? Is running common? Do the younger, smaller, less assertive members of the community get pushed aside? Are there rules about which side to walk? If so, who enforces them and how? How much physical contact is there? What is the nature of that contact?

A similar study of the use of playground space would also reveal something about the culture of the school. I used to work on the fourth floor of an inner city secondary school, from where I could see the infants and junior school playgrounds as well as our own. The infants playground was used by boys and girls quite happily; they played games involving space – skipping, chasing, rounds. They played together and separately. In the junior school playground the sexes were still mixed to some extent, but already the boys were dominating the centre space with a football or two. On our own playground the girls were only visible around the edges, where they sat in groups trying to ignore the central area and its interruptions.

In the rural primary school I attended in Wales in the 1950s girls and boys had separate playgrounds (as well as entrances). There could be some advantage in considering the value of girl/boy only spaces in the play-ground, and in rooms available for use during leisure time. Few would argue that boys and girls should be separated completely, but allowing choice might help some pupils enjoy their leisure time more.

Apart from corridors and playgrounds, the toilets are another area of misery for many pupils. Some pupils use the toilets as the only space that they can really claim as their own. But others, and there are many, avoid using them unless absolutely necessary, or seek to go only in lesson time. Often the basic necessities are missing: toilet paper, soap, towels, mirrors. Many schools have a clear health education policy which the state of the toilets completely contradicts. Often the toilets also lack the privacy which adults would demand as a right. Schools where the toilets are used as an informal common room, should consider what needs are being expressed by pupils, especially by girls, in their use of the toilets.

Schools hold resources which can be used by the wider community, and under Local Management of Schools [LMS] this use will be controlled by the school. The use of buildings and equipment could potentially benefit the wider community as well as giving very clear messages about the values of the school. For example, young mothers form a particularly isolated group in any community. Schools can offer space for mothers to meet and equipment for them to use, learn about or enjoy. Another group of people who might benefit from the use of buildings and equipment are the young. For girls groups to meet in school buildings would be a very positive message for the local community.

3   The physical environment

The values of a school are partly conveyed through the visual environment. Some of this is planned, such as wall displays. Some of it is not – such as graffiti. Planned positive images can have the effect of reinforcing the values which a school wishes to communicate. Finding a speedy remedy for the wrong messages is also important.

4   Administration

All schools have to categorise pupils in the interests of efficient organisation. But such categorisation can convey powerful messages. This is true even at the small-scale level of the individual classroom. On this point school groups could usefully ask some of the questions included in the section at the end of this chapter, which aim to prompt discussion about lists, classroom organisation and pupil consultation.

These are fairly small-scale issues and the changes which might result from asking and answering such questions would be fairly simple to implement. However it must be pointed out that although these are areas where it is easy to open up debate, it can also be easy to open up a minefield, as ingrained practice can become challenged in an uncomfortable way. This will be dealt with later in this chapter.

An institution should also examine the way in which it communicates with the outside world. In what ways are the messages of equality of value and the celebration of diversity actually matched by the language of external communications: letters to parents, handbooks, newspapers etc? Are pupils referred to as a homogenous group of 'he's? How does the school get over the awkwardness of 'your son/daughter' or 'your daughter/son'? What about 'he or she'? or 'she or he'? or 's/he' or 'she/he'? (For a fuller consideration of communications with home, see Chapter 9.)

Does the school refer to parents as though there were always two – and always two of different sexes? Do teachers always refer to 'your Mum' when referring to a parent? Are families – mothers, fathers or others – encouraged to visit the school at times convenient to them? Are home visits encouraged and if so, who is encouraged to make them?

5 The 'hidden curriculum'

The concept of the 'hidden curriculum' is overdue for a new name. It was a useful term when first coined as it referred to an aspect of school life and of pupils' (and adults') learning which was by-and-large unplanned and had escaped rigorous scrutiny and analysis. Since then there have been many valuable examinations of what factors affect pupil outcomes in schools, for example, *15000 Hours*,[8] *Ten Good Schools*,[9] the *Elton Report*,[10] *The School Effect*[11] and recent sociology of education books. It is perhaps more relevant now to refer to the 'para-curriculum' or the 'informal curriculum' which implies less planning, but also that the power to reveal this aspect of pupils' learning is well within our grasp. A phrase which more nearly describes this concept is 'ethos'.

The ethos of a school is expression of the values of the school, expressed both intentionally and unintentionally. For example, the school code of conduct or rules are as much part of the ethos as the manner in which the PE teachers shout their instructions. Many aspects of the school ethos are worth examining for stereotyping. For example: assemblies, speech days and parents' evenings, the manner in which discipline is dispensed, fairness, variation between punishments given to boys and girls. *Genderwatch* Stage Two[12] has a useful list.

Management of change

The management of change is the subject of a huge body of literature in itself. There is no intention to rehearse the work of other writers here, only to draw out some issues for gender and pastoral care.

Gender issues generate many different kinds of reaction: emotional, political, irrational, personal, learned and dismissive. Promoting change in how a school looks at gender issues, in policy on girls and boys, in action in the classroom, in curriculum content, or in organisation of the school will inevitably produce reaction. The first point to remember is that any change will threaten the balance of power within the institution. This might be between the tiers of management, or between pupils and staff or between males and females in the institution. It is not appropriate to ask people to accept a changed power relationship without being able to offer some kind of benefit apart from an ideological one. It seems that gender issues are likely to produced some very extreme reactions; these can be anticipated and responses prepared (see page 30).

The role and attitudes of the headteacher stamp an individual influence on everything that happens or does not happen within the school. Her/his attitude and support is crucial for any attempt to change a school. The headteacher is held responsible for everything that happens in the school, the way in which it is organised, and the way teachers spend their directed time. S/he is obliged to consult the staff on all of this. Since the conditions of employment were imposed in August 1987 headteachers have explicitly been responsible for 'determining and ensuring the implementation of a policy for the pastoral care of the pupils'.

It is therefore worth spending some time considering the role of the headteacher, her/his influence and how progress can be furthered by enlisting her/his support as well as her/his responsibility for pastoral care.

It should be remembered however, that the headteacher is not the only power base within the school. Among most staff groups there are other people who command power through the force of their ideas, morale or personality. These may be the deputy, a head of house or year, a union representative, an established member of staff, the caretaker or another group of people who are vocal and forceful, as well as those groups who exert influence of a quiet variety.

The headteacher and these other power bases can influence decisions on whether gender equity in the school is under discussion, and they can have profound effects on the extent of change which is possible. They can also affect the prevailing attitude within a school. A head who is sympathetic to gender equity will make it much more possible for an institution to be self-critical, to encourage change, and to reward and praise progress. A place to start may be in identifying those who would help, hinder or be neutral in gender work (see page 28).

We frequently have little opportunity to make choices about who the change agent is. In gender issues the difficulty has been that the impetus for change has been the province of a few committed individuals, often with official support, sometimes without it. The weakness of this force was demonstrated during the years of industrial action (1984–8) when in many schools no extra work was done. As a result the working groups or individuals left equal opportunities work to lie fallow and little progress was made. This links with another important point, which will be developed later, about the need to incorporate changes, new practices and reviews into the system so that the lonely innovator at least has the support of the system.

The degree of success experienced by the lonely innovator will depend on her/his status, among other factors. The higher the status, (whether formal or informal) the more chance there is of attracting people's commitment to the notion that change is possible. However some excellent groundwork has been done by individual teachers working in their classrooms – for example on the organisation of the classroom space, ground rules operating, ways in which they encourage non-stereotypical behaviour between pupils and so on. We should not underestimate the effect of the individual teacher on pupils – most of us can remember one or two inspiring teachers from our own schooling. It was often the manner in which they conducted the lessons, and expected their pupils to relate to each other which enhanced the content of the lesson. (See Chapter 4 by Jennifer Walden for more on this.)

The lonely innovator is not an ideal change agent. Institutions are comprised of many individuals and isolated pockets of good practice will not counter the effects of a climate which disadvantages either sex.

Individuals need support, especially if they are taking on the role of change agent. Pressure groups can take many forms; the most common have been the working party and the women's group. The working party model had several disadvantages in that it was often in competition with other working parties (especially multi-cultural/anti-racist working parties), and dependent upon the goodwill of the staff involved. The weakness of this position was exposed during industrial action. With the advent of 'directed time' it may become common to allocate time to this kind of staff involvement in school developments. Unofficial pressure groups have to work against all the disadvantages of being somewhat external to the system.

The most effective change will be that undertaken by the whole community of the school, through discussion, observation and research followed by planned change by teaching and support staff, governors, parents and, of course, the pupils themselves. With so many issues jostling for a place which guarantees attention it is clear that gender and pastoral care issues may not receive high enough priority. However much can be done by a working group or committee which has the official support of the headteacher and governors, and which consults fully with all participants in the school (see Chapter 5).

The temptation and the disappointment of gender-related work is that the issues are so large and the aims so great that there is never a point at which you can say 'this is it'. It is more useful to see work on gender equity as a process than to work with a single aim. Compare this with the introduction of a new syllabus, or administrative arrangement, where review will be required but there is usually a point at which the innovation starts and a point at which it may be seen to be completed. We may even have other ambitions, to change people's attitudes, but this, too, is a chimera. We should not look to change attitudes, but behaviour.

Change that is possible will depend upon the context of the school and will have to be carefully considered. First, there is the internal context. It is difficult, and possibily counter-productive, to change some aspects of the school. For example, many teachers find that lists which are divided into boys (first) then girls, reinforce the idea that the division between the sexes should be repeated at all levels of the organisation. As a result this is one of those things which many institutions have changed. But while it may be easy in one institution to change a simple thing such as the order of form lists and registers, in another school the entrenched position of a few may make it hard. In one school it was only when the school roll was computerised, and lists could therefore be produced in any order– males, females, by age, by date of birth or any other combination – that the office staff finally agreed that they could still compile Form 7 despite the registers and form lists being produced in one alphabetical order. The concerns of the teachers, the parents, the governors, the support staff and the pupils themselves need to be considered.

Second, the external context also needs to be considered. How well will proposed changes fit with LEA policy? What support will be available (see Chapter 3)? What about the prevailing political climate locally and nationally – how will that affect what you are trying to do?

It will also be necessary to consider what resources are available to help achieve your aims. What time, people, money, skills are required and available? What incentives are you able to offer?

Building change, review and evaluation in the system

Changing practice in the area of gender equity and pastoral care is so dauntingly large a task that it is vital that change is marked and celebrated. In one school the convening of a gender working party was greeted with sighs and weariness because, it was said, all the discussion had taken place before with no result. The chair of the working group went back to the minutes and recommendations of the previous group and found that all but one of its recommendations had been implemented. But they had gone unremarked and progress had not been acknowledged, so pessimism had set in.

Monitoring is an essential part of marking and recognising change, and also important in pointing the way forward and in reviewing strategies adopted. Monitoring can be built into the process in several ways: by including it in equal opportunities job specifications; by building reviewing and monitoring into a programme of action; by intermittent sampling; by systematic collection of statistics and other data.

Change needs to be sustained by continuous pressure to prevent an institution from reverting to previous practice. There is a need to incorporate change, to make it part of the system. Some suggestions for this are to create equal opportunities posts, to write equal opportunities briefs into job specifications, to make equal opportunities work a regular part of the school's reviewing procedure, to make equal opportunities work a regular agenda item for meetings of year/house teams, pastoral postholders, the senior management team, school and year councils, and governors' meetings.

Conclusion

Successfully changing pupils' experience of pastoral care and gender equity in schools requires the staff to engage in open discussion and to arrive at broad agreement about what are understood to be the aims of the school in these matters. Change can be effected by a number of different groupings and on a range of different aspects of school life, but will only be sustained if ways are found to build change into the system. The most effective change of all occurs when we can open our debates to involve the young people for whose personal and social development we hold considerable responsibility.

Things to do

1 Recruitment and status

Useful questions to ask are:

1 Do the number and status of men and women in my school reflect the usual pattern?
2 Do the number and status of men and women in the pastoral structure of the school reflect the same pattern as in the school as a whole? If not, in what ways is it different? Does that tell me anything about the school's conception of pastoral care and gender?
3 Does the school/authority have any policy about the recruitment of women to senior positions? What could be done to recruit more women in to senior positions in pastoral care? Do all jobs advertised have clear job descriptions and candidate specifications? [See Chapter 3 for more on this.]

A common pattern in schools is for most teachers to take on the role of form tutor. Usually there are a few teachers who are excused these responsibilities. If there are more members of staff than required to fill this role you might reasonably ask these questions:

1 What criteria are used to establish exemptions?
2 Is there a balance in the sexes of those who are exempted? Can this be explained by reference to the criteria?

2 Positive and negative

The aim of the activity (also known as force-field analysis) is to identify those individuals and groups who will help or hinder any change you might want to make.

Take a piece of paper, and divide it in two. On the top half write all the names of the people and groups who will help move you forward. On the lower half of the page place all those who will have a negative effect.

Now do the same activity for other factors which might help or hinder (eg LEA policy, support group outside school, allied initiatives, HMI Report, initiative fatigue etc).

Now discuss with a friend and supporter where your main support lies and how you are going to utilise it. You need to take account of the negative factors, but you are not trying to persuade those who appear on the lower half of your first sheet. Your main effort should be directed at all the people who do not appear on either half.

3 Administration

Here school groups could usefully ask some of the following questions:

1 How are form lists and registers ordered? Does this give first place to either sex? If so, what purpose does this serve? If there is a purpose to be served, can it be met in a different way? With computer-aided administration, is it not possible to organise information so that it can be reproduced in any classification required: age, address, primary school, gender etc.
2 How do we organise each group within the classroom and outside? Do classes line up, boys and girls separately? If so, what purpose does this serve? If there is a purpose can it be served in any other way? Do pupils leave the classroom in any particular order? If so, does this give first place to either sex? If so, is there a purpose to be served in this? Could this purpose be better served in any other way?
3 How do we organise pupils within the classroom? Who decides the

seating arrangement – pupils or teacher? If teacher, does s/he seat boys and girls separately, or in mixed groups? If the pupils decide, how do they arrange themselves? Is this having any unintended effects on the work and relationships of the class? Is there an alternative which could assist the learning atmosphere in the classroom?

4   Do girls or boys take the greater share of time spent using equipment? If there is a bias how has this arisen and is there any practice which could assist a fair or compensatory sharing of the use of equipment (eg a rota for the computer)?

5   Which sex does more of the helping and enabling tasks of the classroom eg giving out books, fetching equipment etc. What does this say about that group (is it a repeat of the 'two strong lads, two helpful tidy girls' syndrome)? Could a better way of sharing and involving all pupils in these tasks be arrived at, eg by a monitor rota?

6   Have the pupils been consulted on any of the above issues?

4   Space

The aim of this activity is to identify who uses the space in the school.

Choose three places in the school (eg playground, entrance hall, assembly areas, wherever pupils organise the space for themselves) and monitor use of the space.

In a pastoral team or other meeting consider this situation and discuss possible resolutions:

> *Lesley Smith was often late for lessons, arriving several minutes after the rest of the class. Lesley was the least assertive member of the form and often the butt of jokes or the victim of bullying by other class members, although outside the classroom she seemed isolated and quiet. After numerous referrals for lateness, Lesley's form tutor tackled her about it. Lesley maintained that she proceeded as quickly as she could from lesson to lesson and shrugged when asked why then she was so often behind the others. The tutor decided to observe Lesley's behaviour, and following afternoon registration followed her progress to the next lesson. Instead of taking the same route as her classmates Lesley took a long rout, mostly outside despite the rain. Lesley did proceed quickly, but the route was so long that she did indeed arrive late. When confronted with this Lesley admitted that she hated the corridors, she got jostled, punched, teased, had her things taken. All this was fairly good natured, but difficult for her to put up with.*

In fact Lesley was helped when the tutor appointed travelling companions to accompany Lesley and she became more confident and punctual.

5 Male/female monitoring

Make a statistical analysis of any of the following by sex:

a   option take-up by subject;
b   examination entry;
c   examination results;
d   suspensions;
e   referrals to outside agencies;
f   form monitors;
g   lateness;
h   absence.

Publish your results and ask for comments.

6 Inset

Packs of materials for staff development include:

a) Carter, A.; Magee, F.; Mapp, L.; Myers, K.; Rospigliosi, R. and Watkins, C. (1983) *Equal Opportunities: what's in it for boys?* ILEA/ Schools Council 1983. Whyld Publishing Co-op 1986. Moorland House, Caistor, Lincs, LN7 6SF.
b) Carter, A. et al (1986) *Changing Places* (Materials focusing on new pupils). ILEA/Schools Council and Whyld Publishing Co-op.
c) Hannan, G. (1991) *Outcomes – Equal Opportunities: Gender.* Blackwell.

7 Responses

Not everyone welcomes change. How would you deal with the following responses:

It's that bunch of women again! is a dismissive response.

I'm not going to change what I've done all my teaching career because of working party recommendations is a conservative approach which suggests that the speaker feels no ownership of the changes suggested, and sees them as undermining of familiar routines.

Why are we wasting our time on these fringe issues when we should be spending time on. . .(the current pressing concern)? This response suggests that gender issues are not central to education and that there are more urgent priorities.

It's just Ms X's power trip. She'll be moving on soon, and then where will we be with this? This is a common response to a lonely innovator.

References

1 Watkins, C. (1985) 'Does Pastoral Care = Personal and Social Education?' in *Pastoral Care in Education*. Vol 3, No 3.
2 NAPCE (1986) *Preparing for Pastoral Care – In-Service Training for the Pastoral Aspect of the Teacher's Role* Blackwell.
3 HMI (1990) *Pastoral Care in Secondary Schools: an inspection of some aspects of pastoral care in 1987–88*. DES.
4 Weightman, J. (1989) 'Women in Management' *Educational Management and Administration* 17.
5 NAPCE (1984) *Initial Training for the Pastoral Aspect of the Teacher's Role*.
6 National Curriculum Council (1989).
7 Marland, M. 'The Pastoral Curriculum' in Best, R., Jarvis, C. and Ribbins, P. (eds.) *Perspectives on Pastoral Care* Heinemann.
8 Rutter et al (1979) *15000 Hours* Open Books.
9 DES (1977) *Matters for Discussion 1: Ten Good Schools* HMI Discussion Paper.
10 DES (1989) *Discipline in Schools*; report of the Commission of Enquiry chaired by Lord Elton.
11 Smith and Tomlinson (1989) *The School Effect: a study of multi-racial comprehensives* Policy Studies Institute.
12 Myers, K. (1987) *Genderwatch* SCDC.

Further reading

Sex equality and the pastoral curriculum – a pack of activities to use in tutor time. ILEA Spencer Park Teachers' Centre, 1984.
Steps to equality, the report of the Primary Gender Equality Working Party. London Borough of Brent Education Department, 1985.

3
An equal opportunities employer?: A role for the Local Education Authority?

Lesley Kant

Introduction

Farmshire is an equal opportunities employer.

Newtown is an equal opportunities employer and welcomes applications from people regardless of their sex, ethnic background, disability, sexual orientation...

Local government is a major source of employment in the United Kingdom and such statements are familiar trailers to many local education authority job advertisements. Whether or not they encourage minorities to apply for the posts is less certain.

Approximately one-eighth of the total labour force is employed in local government; almost two-thirds of this are women.[1] Stone's survey shows that of the 11.6 million women employed by local government, most are found in low status and poorly-paid employment, are likely to be concentrated in the educational and social services and in particular occupational groups, and almost one million of these are employed part-time.[2]

The local education authority is the largest service in local government, responsible for services which may range from playgroups and nursery classes through to further continuing education. It has a statutory responsibility to ensure that it carries out its duties and functions with regard both to national legislation and any local policy agreements. Its pastoral responsibility for equal opportunities covers employment, educational and developmental roles; including:

- the recruitment and retention of staff, ensuring that employment legislation is met;
- care and support for employees in terms of good equal opportunities practice: this includes officers, teachers, inspectors, cleaners, caretakers, school meals staff and office workers;
- the curriculum of schools and colleges in terms of sex discrimination and educational legislation and statutory guidance.

These pastoral responsibilities require clear policies to be effective, including policies as an employer of direct labour and as a body responsible for providing an educational service.

Legislative requirements

Educational and employment legislation affects these pastoral responsibilities in a number of ways.

Equal opportunities in education has been enshrined in long standing legislation. The 1944 Education Act is still significant, for it was the first occasion that 'equality of opportunity' was defined in statute. The Act encouraged the fulfilment of potential, but equality of opportunity was defined largely in terms of age, ability and class (extending the rights of the individual to schooling as opposed to the rights of groups). Later, educational commissions such as Newsom and Robbins began to acknowledge the changing role of girls and women, but it was not until the Equal Pay and Sex Discrimination Acts of 1970 and 1975 that the elimination of gender discrimination became a statutory responsibility.

The *Equal Pay Act* entitles women doing the same or broadly similar work as men and working for the same employer to the same rates of pay and other employment conditions. The Equal Pay Amendment (1984) sought to strengthen this legislation. It introduced the concept of equal value: thus a woman may claim equal pay with a man when her work is of equal value to his in terms of the demand the work makes on her in areas such as effort, skills and decision making. The original Act had little direct effect on schools – for teachers had achieved equal pay by the 1960s. However, the amendment has some scope to help women teachers and possibly other female employees. It allows a person to claim a comparison with an employee at a different location but covered by common conditions of service. Thus, in principle, a female head of home economics can claim that her responsibilities in terms of staff supervision, curriculum provision and maintenance of work stations compares fully with a male CDT specialist: a female head of girls' PE could claim work of equal value with a male head of boys' PE. Sadly, since the amendment was introduced, few claims have been decided. 'The complexity of the law is such' (some would say deliberately) 'that few legal advisers, and even fewer employers and trade union officials, can hope to understand what is going on.' (*Guardian* 1987)

The *Sex Discrimination Act* (1975) was significant and has probably had a greater effect than is sometimes appreciated. It rendered sex discrimination unlawful in employment, training and related matters and established the concept of both direct and indirect discrimination.

1   Direct discrimination is largely concerned with attitudes: it means treating a woman less favourably than a man because she is a woman; for example, preferring to appoint a male teacher or caretaker because it is wrongly assumed that parents prefer men in such posts.
2   Indirect discrimination tends to derive from structures rather than attitudes, but, in principle, should be easier to overcome. Conditions which are likely to favour one sex more than the other should not be used: an age ceiling for a post might be an example of indirect discrimination. Predictably, women are more likely than men to take time out of paid employment for child bearing and child rearing: this, in turn, means they are unlikely to be able to comply with age requirements such as 40 for a deputy headship and 30–35 for a middle management post.

Educationally, the most important aspect of the 1975 Act was Section 22, which challenged the status quo provision of education and established the right of equal access to educational facilities and equality of treatment for girls and boys within co-educational schools. It made it illegal for schools to offer certain subjects to boys or girls only; even the notion of opting in – for example a girl opting to join a boys' craft class – is an example of less favourable treatment because the onus is on the girl to make a special application to join the class or group. This would, of course, also apply to a boy who wished to join a home economics or dance class. This tension between curriculum access and equality of educational experience has been partly overtaken by the National Curriculum and the concept of pupil entitlement, though entitlement may prove more elusive than anticipated.[3]

The 1975 Act also makes it unlawful to use sex as a criterion in terms of allocating places to schools, classes or groups. Quotas, therefore (whether for entry to selective schools or to achieve sexual balance within a group or school) are illegal, as Birmingham discovered by not providing as many places for girls in its grammar schools as for boys. As an employer and a provider of education, an LEA has a duty to ensure that these requirements are met. The implications of this are considered in more detail later.

LEAs had to move speedily to keep up with the educational legislation of the 1980s. The 1986 Act was rendered almost obsolete by the 1988 Education Reform Act. Neither the 1986 nor the 1988 Education Acts specifically addressed the issue of gender, but both have considerable implications for local educational administration and, indirectly, for equal opportunities. The legislation increased the responsibility for school governors in terms of staffing and management through local financial management provision. This makes it more difficult for an LEA to maintain consistent and coherent procedures in terms of staffing and employment practices. The 1986 Act allows school governors to determine their school curriculum in terms of sex education (and religious education, depending on whether the school is a voluntary 'church' school).

The 1988 Education Reform Act seized central control of the curriculum by establishing a national and basic curriculum which must be offered to all pupils in compulsory education.

The school curriculum must be broad and balanced and must promote the spiritual, moral, cultural, mental and physical development of pupils within schools and society in general; it must prepare pupils for the opportunities, responsibilities and experiences of adult life. Apart from the ten foundation subjects and religious education, it is envisaged that there will be opportunities to explore other curriculum areas. In a letter to the newly established National Curriculum Council, the then Secretary of State, Kenneth Baker, asked the Council to address the issues of equal opportunities and multicultural education.[4]

The 1988 Act also requires LEAs to have a policy on the curriculum and to keep this under review. The LEA's curriculum policy must encompass the basic curriculum but can be broader and more challenging as well as responsive to local needs and cultures.

An LEA is required to ensure that all its employees understand and implement the legislation and ensure that discriminatory practices are challenged. The increased responsibility of school governors must be taken on board by the LEA: governors need guidance and training to ensure that they understand national legislation and the LEA's policies and are aware of their responsibilities, such as staffing and employment procedures. Given that the LEA's statutory responsibility for employment remains despite increased governors' powers in appointment of staffing, this development and training role is of critical importance.

All teachers need to be fully aware of national and local policies and curriculum requirements. This implies more than information giving. Effective understanding will require a range of support – consultation, debate and documentation – which clearly sets out the LEA's expectations; a regular programme of INSET, including school-based opportunity; distance learning; networking and opportunities for people to come together and explore thinking.

LEA policies – real or lip service?

Policies must be agreed if procedures are to be formalised. EOC research makes it clear that informality plays a major role in propping up discriminatory practices and can lead to 'inconsistent, secretive and unaccountable practices which create the climate in which discrimination occurs.' (EOC 1988).

The growing awareness of equal opportunities in local authorities has led many to adopt policies in this field. This, in turn, has led to the use of proselytising messages on job advertisements. Some LEAs give the equal opportunities banner little more than lip service. Some statements have been agreed following periods of negotiation with the local government unions, and understanding of the implications of such policy may be a long way off or unsought. Other LEAs may use the term without any explicit policy; intriguingly, a third of those with a policy do not use such statements on job advertisements! Given a judgement against Lancashire LEA – one of the earliest authorities to use the phrase 'equal opportunities employer', this may be judicious. An industrial tribunal held that the authority was guilty of discrimination in employment and that a deputy headteacher had been subject to discriminatory treatment in headship appointments.[5]

It is worth noting that when the ILEA moved into a formal policy of monitoring applications and appointments by sex and race and potential candidates began to see the principle enshrined in practice, then it secured greater response from female applicants. By the time the ILEA was disbanded, almost 50% of its headteachers were female.[6]

Many feminists have argued that policy statement, along with legislation, are academic and little use in practice. However, they can be an important staging point in the achievement of equality. Those who are involved in the policy formulation usually become better informed and, therefore, their consciousness is raised. Policies can legitimise the activities of those already committed and active in the field and may deter those who would otherwise discredit good practice; policies can create the climate in which change is more likely to come about. As with legislation, policies have the potential 'to force change whether or not the reasons for doing so are accepted and understood'.[7]

In Andrew Cant's description of Manchester's progress in this field he notes 'If LEA policy is to be more than a paper exercise it needs translating into practical action in the schools themselves' and he describes the gap between defining policy and effecting change.[8] Although he believes that policy agreements get the issue firmly on the agenda, whether it remains there owes much to the support of politicians and senior officers in the Authority.

In learning and teaching, policy declarations may help by defining the strength of the Authority's commitment and by clarifying the parameters of the curriculum. The ultimate test lies in the practical and day-to-day activities of the classroom. Many schools and teachers will use LEA policy to support their work in this field and, to be effective, they need to work through for themselves the range of curriculum implications. It would be unusual nowadays not to find committed teachers in many schools with a clear understanding of sex stereotyping and sexism within the planned curriculum and pastoral provision. The search is for a way in which they can be helped to implement their thinking both within their school and with other teachers across the authority. As Carol Adams suggests 'the more committed the women teachers, the less relevant they believed policy to be. Their real concern was with action and implementation.' (Adams 1987)[9]

Other staff may still need to be encouraged by senior management teams; senior managers may in turn need to be encouraged by LEA officers to address the issue. Not merely the curriculum content, but the ways in which schools are organised and staffed; the ways in which people work together and talk; the ways in which behaviour is transmitted and pupils addressed; these need also to be challenged.[10]

Good practice

A local authority concerned to ensure gender is on the agenda and effective in practice should explore the following issues:

Policy

The establishment of an equal opportunities policy across the whole of the authority is an essential pre-requisite. 57% of authorities with a policy had a written statement varying from a single line to a 144–page document (EOC 1988). Some authorities recognise this by ensuring that committee papers address equal opportunities implications as a matter of course; such a requirement focuses the mind of officers and ensures the issue stays on the political and resources agenda. It is a subtle means of educating officers as well as members.

Responsible officer

The appointment of an Equal Opportunities Officer who is responsible for co-ordinating gender and possibly race issues and dealing with specific areas such as training, legislation and monitoring as well as support is often advanced as an important step forward. However, such a post is capable of marginalisation. Isabella Stone's study for the EOC makes it clear that the grade, the budget, the administrative support and the location of such an officer has considerable implications for the role's effectiveness in practice (EOC 1988).

Working parties

The setting up of a working party across departments with a wide-ranging composition and including elected members can play a critical role in support and form a means of translating principles into practice. Again, the same EOC survey has suggested that success in operating equal opportunities policies is highly dependent on member intervention.

Advisory team

The appointment of an educational adviser with specific responsibilities can ensure that the issue remains on the educational agenda. However, it is important to ensure commitment from *all* members of the advisory service and that the appointment of a specific person does not polarise the issue, dilute the power base and ensure that officers and advisers assume that they need do more than pay lip service. Brent, ILEA, Haringey and Coventry were some of the first authorities to set up appointments in the field. In Brent, the adviser had a specific monitoring responsibility and the right to attend interviews for headship appointments – a clear example of affirmative action in practice. In ILEA the Inspector was a senior member of the inspectorate, commensurate with other senior staff inspectors with subject or cross-curricular briefs. By targeting teacher professional development as a critical route for ensuring the effectiveness of ILEA's policy, the postholder did much to ensure that practical developments in schools and colleges took place.

School guidelines

Schools and coleges require clear guidance which makes explicit the legislative requirements (practical guidance on the implications of the Sex Discrimination, Equal Pay Acts and amendments) as well as the curricular, organisational and pedagogic implications of the legislation. This needs to be expressed in language that is accessible and clarifies the LEA's expectations of the schools.

Curriculum and pastoral policy

A general curriculum and pastoral policy statement is a important means of enshrining equal opportunities within the mainstream educational framework of the authority. The Education Acts of 1986 and 1988 require an LEA to be clear about its curricular direction. The Education Reform Act also requires LEAs to ensure that the effective implementation of the National Curriculum requirements and equal opportunities can be considered as an integral part of all curricular areas. This may require an overall curriculum document as well as more detailed guidelines in the full range of curriculum areas. This is timely, given that curriculum areas such as home economics, business studies, economics and CDT are being reworked and redefined as Technology in the National Curriculum.

Language

The way in which the LEA's documentation is written can also have a bearing on the way it is interpreted. Legislation frustratingly still uses 'he' and 'his' but there is absolutely no reason why local authority documentation has to reflect this sexist use of language. Headteacher, s/he, her/his, should be commonly used terms, just as 'synthetic' and 'artificial' for 'man-made' and the study of 'people' or 'humanity' for study of 'man' are easy but important ways of ensuring that language is sensitive to the issue.

Recruitment and selection

This is one of the most contentious areas and probably where the most persistent discrimination operates. Recruitment and selection procedures need to be clear and unbiased. A job description and person specification can be a means of clarifying the job expectation and accountabililty, and can enable officers to ensure that hidden assumptions relating to the post do not come into play. Particular experience and specific qualifications also need to be fully discussed and agreed – as takes place in those states in the USA which operate affirmative action policies.

a) Advertisements

The advertisements for the post and the place where they can be read can also be significant. There is considerable belief in the Afro-Carribean and Asian communities that advertisements which have been placed in ethnic papers generate a higher degree of response from blacks. Certainly, the wording of 'equal opportunities employer' and, indeed, the rather more specific encouragement offered in some local authorities may be a start.

Encouragement is particularly important and it is not illegal to encourage minorities, thus,

Jane Jones, previous deputy head, had left to take up a headship with another authority. We are looking for an equally well-qualified and experienced person to take her place, and *Applications from women are particularly welcomed* are publicly acceptable when the employer is looking to redress the balance.

Nothing, however, encourages so much as example. ILEA's affirmative policy on headteachers' appointments during the early 1980s not only resulted in increased appointments of women – it encouraged women to apply in greater numbers than before and eliminated the vicious circle of few women applicants. Nothing discourages more than failure. Evidence suggests that women are more diffident than men in application terms. Female role models remain few; women tend to value work for its intrinsic worth rather than status and hierarchical achievement. Counselling and encouragement help women who are often more diffident and modest about their abilities and potential than men.[11]

b) Application forms
Form filling can also be a form of unconscious bias. Many forms still require marital status and details of former names – often described as 'maiden'.

c) Selection procedures
Careful use of the person specification and post description is critical. Careful monitoring should take place to ensure that conscious or unconscious bias does not percolate through the sifting process. If the authority is genuine about its commitment to recruiting women – particularly in more senior posts and in non-traditional areas – it may need to be positive in terms of reviewing female applications. This works both ways, of course. Just as I was dismayed to discover a colleague had a tendency to weed out any applications in which the Ms was used as a prefix, so another administrator declined to take up references on a perfectly well qualified male secretary on the grounds that the typing pool supervisor would not fancy working with a man in her team. Selection criteria can be guilty of indirect discrimination; age ceilings for a post need to be very carefully evaluated for their relevance before being applied. Price v Civil Service Commission secured a ruling that an age ceiling could discriminate unfairly by making women ineligible for certain civil service posts because their time out for child rearing and child bearing would mean they would have difficulty in acquiring the relevant experience. Thus, an authority which applied a

ceiling of 40 to deputy headship appointments could be operating indirect discrimination.

d) Appropriate experience
'Appropriate experience' for senior teaching posts could view varied experience in one school as equivalent as varied experience in a range of schools. Women's mobility is still limited and the structural reasons for this – the pattern of child bearing and rearing and male primacy in terms of work – need to be recognised in employment before it can be overcome, or women will be doubly disadvantaged.

e) Interviewing arrangements
Interviews should enable candidates to relax and offer their best. Interview guidelines and training are essential to ensure that sexist questions are eliminated. Should a biased question emerge from an uninformed person, the panel should intervene. When a question on child care responsibilities was asked recently in my presence, I intervened to say (i) it didn't have to be answered and, (ii) all the male candidates would also be questioned in like vein. I can still remember the bemusement on the faces and verbal incoherence of the three men when they were asked if they intended to increase the size of their families and what arrangements they made regarding their children while they were away at work.

Criteria for the post in hand also need to be specific. In practice most interviews tend to be normative. People are compared with other people. The truism 'the right person for the right job' may mean looking to see whether the person can fit in to a team. This may also ensure that like people recruit like people: while the norm is white and middle class and male, then this is also a convenient short circuit for maintaining the numbers of white middle class males in employment.

Training and development

Procedures such as those described above need to be underwritten by an effective programme of development for all involved in selection and recruitment. It has already been stressed that training for governors is particularly critical, given the increased power of governing bodies under the 1986 and 1988 Acts. The Education Reform Act shifts much executive responsibility to schools and heads and minimises the role of the LEA in the appointment system. A comprehensive programme of governor and headteacher training must be a major priority and, to be effective, needs documentary guidance.

Advisory and inspectorate service

> Since equal opportunities is best understood as a process and not
> a product, it follows that the way the advisory team itself works
> should be scrutinised. (Myers 1988)

Inspectors and advisers should never minimise the extent of their influence. Although their powers are minimal, their capacity to create
climates, encourage good practice and challenge bad practice, and to alert
teachers to important issues is considerable. The composition of the advisory team and its own way of working are equally important elements in the
promotion of equal opportunities. As Kate Myers has also said 'Messages
are picked up from the way we behave towards others as well as the
practices and procedures we adopt'.

Unpublished research by Ann Williamson of the University of East
Anglia reveals that, where male advisers were guilty of sexism in their
behaviour patterns, this was recognised by many women in schools, who
felt significantly undermined by the attitudes. Exhortation and encouragement are important ways in which people can change and develop, but
monitoring and vigilance may also be needed to ensure that people are
forced to think again about their patterns of behaviour.

Monitoring

An LEA needs to be continually vigilant and to monitor and evaluate the
quality of the education service. Monitoring is a means of gathering information in order to change policy and ensure objectives are effected.
Monitoring of staff employment patterns, recruitment procedures and
absentee rates yields useful information about the way in which the authority manages itself. It also signals the importance attached to the issues it
addresses. Norfolk LEA was committed to ensuring equality in terms of
INSET participation. Its rather patchy data-system suggested that men in
the 25–45 year age range picked up the largest share of the available
long-term INSET resources; that women were the major participants in
Teacher Centre activity (usually at twilight and without travel and subsist-
ence). As a result, Norfolk began monitoring by sex and age as well as
phase and provenance, to ensure the cake was more evenly distributed.

Monitoring is often viewed with suspicion, but it can be a sensitive
instrument in detecting inequality and providing for redress. Thus an LEA
committed to equal distribution of resources which puts secondary education at the forefront of curriculum and professional development funding
will find itself indirectly discriminating against women because they are
under-represented in the secondary phase.

Employment practice

Attitudes are important but structures can also be discriminatory. LEAs should consider adopting a range of structures which encourage women and provide them with the opportunities to achieve. Such structures include

- flexible working hours;
- job sharing and child care support;
- strategies to encourage married women returners not only to come back into teaching but to be appropriately retrained so that they can compete on equal terms;
- career breaks for both men and women;
- paternity and maternity leave.

These are all important means of recognising that women in general undertake two jobs. Such provision does signal that an authority is taking the issue of being an 'equal opportunities *employer*' seriously.

Looking forward

Kate Myers suggests that there are three major reasons behind LEAs adopting equal opportunities strategies:

1 Recognition that resources (female human resources) are not being properly exploited;
2 Political commitment, often from members through political manifestos;
3 Grass roots pressure from those active in the field and in the classroom. (Myers 1988).

Isabella Stone's study for the EOC suggests that to be effective, support for the policy from elected members is critical and effectiveness of officers is hampered without this support. Undoubtedly LEA officers have a difficult and sometimes unrewarding job of persuading members; likewise some members will also have the challenging task of developing their officers. Analysis of those LEAs which have introduced policies suggests that political commitment is more likely to have been the driving force than professional judgment: in other words, members educating officers rather than officers persuading members. This may be more a statement of the distribution of power than distribution of commitment. Officers may sometimes need to be pragmatic and issues such as resources exploitation may prove a more cogent argument that equity as a means of persuasion.

The way in which education has evolved in this country means that it is difficult to legislate for some aspects of educational provision. Teachers have an unusual degree of professional autonomy. Although current educational initiatives in INSET and teacher appraisal, classroom and collaborative approaches to curriculum development have encouraged many teachers to open the doors of their classroom and to work as a team, this is not the norm. Some classroom activity may reinforce sexist and racist attitudes; it is unlikely for there to be real improvement until the classroom becomes the forum for change. This suggests an active and open educational partnership between the LEA, the school, the teacher, the parent and the pupil.

This tension is echoed in child-centred education approaches, particularly as pioneered by many of the great early-years protagonists, such as Froebel and Rachel McMillan. The class teacher who works with her reception class from their individual and corporate interests may find that gender stereotypes are already entrenched at an early age. Rudduck and May's 1983 study of *Sex Stereotyping and the Early Years*[12] revealed widespread sex stereotyping by very young boys and girls: boys' dominance in the classroom and playground and in terms of harassing behaviour was widespread. Unpublished research by Jill Shea at the University of East Anglia has discovered controlling language used by very young boys against girls. Such evidence may not persuade LEAs to change early years policy but they will want the issues to be explored and the implications understood and addressed by teachers.

Much recent educational writing has focused on low morale amongst teachers and difficulties in recruitment. The local administration of an education service is also vulnerable in the current climate of dynamic educational legislation and central direction. The Education Reform Act, the national curriculum and local financial management undermine the concept of a local education authority: its ability to manage change is lessened when its executive responsibility is diminished. Other pressures, such as the government's emphasis on competition in the work place, and market forces, have also made it difficult for an LEA to take a greater role in addressing equal opportunities in terms of contract compliance – successfully pioneered by the ILEA in the early 1980s. Competitive tendering has meant that it is more difficult for an LEA to ensure equal opportunities in staffing and employment in a number of service areas. Nevertheless, a local authority will continue to be a major recruiter and employer. It will continue to need to train its workforce effectively and, as such, it needs to anticipate future employment trends and to try to ensure that its management system is not only equitable but sensitive to patterns of change.

Most demographic forecasting suggests that a revolution in the workplace is under way in terms of hours at work, the place of work and cycles of work. This has implications not only for those who have traditionally given up work to bear children and raise a family, but for their partners and their children. An LEA in the 1990s needs to have courage to be equitable, but to be successful it may need to be radical both in its employment structures and in its curriculum provision. It needs to anticipate the future with vision and confidence; to ensure that it espouses values which foster a motivated, committed and fairly treated workforce.

Decreasing numbers of young people leaving school in the early 1990s will mean a drop in unemployment and recruitment difficulties for employers. LEAs are already finding considerable problems in both recruiting and retaining their teaching force at a time of considerable stress because of radical change and poor pay. There will be a need to make more use of older workers and flexible patterns of work and sensitive attitudes to the workforce will be essential; the young will be able to pick and choose work. As a major employer as well as the body responsible for generating positive attitudes through education and training, the role of the LEA will be critical. An LEA which reviews and revitalises its pastoral role and becomes a real equal opportunities employer will be better placed to meet the future with success.

References

1 Equal Opportunities Commission (EOC) (1988) *Local Authority Equal Opportunities Policies: Report and Survey by the EOC*. EOC, Manchester.

2 Stone (1988) *Equal Opportunities in Local Authorities: Developing effective strategies for the implementation of policies for women*. HMSO.

3 Kant, L. (1987) 'National Curriculum – Notionally Equal' *Education Review*. October 1987, NUT.

4 DES (1988) Remit letter from Secretary of State to Chairman of National Curriculum Council. 26/8/88.

5 EOC (1986) *Chadwick v LCC* Report of Industrial Tribunal judgment. EOC, Manchester.

6 Longman (1989) *Education Year Book*.

7 Carr, L. (1985) in Whyte, J. et al. *Girl-Friendly Schooling* Methuen.

8 Cant, A. (1985) in Whyte, J. et al. *Girl-Friendly Schooling* Methuen.

9 Adams, C. (1987) 'Teacher Attitudes to Issues of Sex Equality' in Whyte et al. *Girl Friendly Schooling*.

10 Myers K. (1988) 'Putting gender on the agenda' *Perspective* NAIEA Journal.

11 Watts, T. and Kant, L. (1986) *A Working Start* SCDC Longman.

12 May, N. and Ruddock, J. (1983) *Sex stereotyping and the early years of schooling*. Available from Centre for Applied Research in Education, University of East Anglia.

4

Gender issues in classroom organisation and management

Jennifer Walden

In addressing issues in classrooms, the first section of this chapter presents a wider view of schooling and social inequality, with the main focus on gender. This is necessary in order to avoid too simple a view of classrooms, in isolation from the wider context and its effects. It is important to guard against an unrealistic view of classrooms and equal opportunities work and to ensure that we do not 'set teachers up' for disappointment by offering just as unrealistic a view of the possibilities for change.

Introduction

This chapter is concerned with strategies to alleviate gender inequalities in the classroom. The issue of inequalities in education and equal opportunities action to combat these has been with us for some years. Particularly from the late 70s teachers and researchers identified inequalities of gender and race in our education system, where previously they were understood almost wholly in terms of social class.[1]

Since that time a great deal of work has been done on equal opportunities at a number of levels. Local education authorities have produced policies and appointed personnel with specific equal opportunity responsibilities. Schools, through varying structures, have established equal opportunities issues as a recognisable concern and have worked towards equal opportunity goals in a number of specific areas. Equality of opportunity is written into the contract of educational initiatives like TVEI; even in the implementation of the Education Reform Act, although it has not been central to its concerns, there is an acknowledgement of the importance of equal opportunities, across the curriculum.

Central and local government policy does not guarantee change in the classroom, to which a number of 'embattled' teachers will testify. As with all educational issues and policy applications, it is at the day-to-day level of the classroom that wider-ranging propositions are tested out. It is important to maintain an overview of education and equal opportunities, in order to contextualise that classroom practice. The first section of this chapter seeks to provide a frame of reference for those issues which seem to relate in specific ways to the classroom.

Section One examines some important ideas about social inequality, before addressing equality of opportunity in education. This leads to consideration of how schools can contribute to equal opportunities and provides a context for Section Two to examine the classroom in detail.

Social inequality

Inequality in our society means that some people have more economic resources than others and have access to further actual and potential resources.

Historically, women have been – and still are – considered unequal to men. Sexism can affect men, but women suffer the effects of sexism to a vastly greater extent than men. Stereotypical judgements are made of women's inferiority, on the basis of their sex. This position of inferiority is socially constructed: it is accompanied by ideas, attitudes and practices which privilege male-gendered over female-gendered attributes, stereotype and denigrate female capabilities and variously define and thereby seek to regulate female sexuality.

Sexism permeates women's everyday experience and continually reinforces and articulates male power over female. The combination of sexism and racism is complex in its effects on black women and girls. Where all women face stereotypes which denigrate their status and seek to control their sexuality, black females suffer further and particular denigrating and 'controlling' stereotypes and denial of economic status, because they are black. While the stereotypes differ for Afro-Caribbean and Asian women and girls the racism underlying them is the same.[2]

Given that these inequalities exist and persist in our society, how does education relate to them? A variety of answers may be given. They direct our attention to the school's role in combating inequality.

Social inequality and educational inequality

There are different views on how and how far education functions, through its 'social regulation', to maintain social division and stratification. Historically, many ideas about education and educational reforms have been based

47

on the understanding that men and women will (and should!) fill distinctly different positions in society.[3]

However, it cannot be said that education can *guarantee* particular regulative effects and outcomes through its processes. Certainly education cannot automatically reproduce positions in the economy or dominant ideas in the school population.

In the latter half of this century education reform has invoked the promise of undermining social stratification, through individual enhancement. This has been its outward expression of intent and rationale.

Equality of opportunity

There is a fundamental belief, enshrined in the 1944 Education Act, that through educational achievement – understood primarily in terms of the acquisition of educational qualifications – an individual's life chances can be enhanced, regardless of that individual's acscribed unequal social position.

The development of concern about inequality in educational terms occurred when it was understood that certain groups in society received a different kind of education which led to greater life chances. Comprehensive education was expected to change this educational inequality by providing all state educated young people with the same kind of education.

However what emerged from this expansionist, 'equal equals the same kind' philosophy in the 1970s was that the inequalities existing at the outset, in people's differentiated social positions, continued to be reflected in their educational outcomes. As group, the working class, girls and black people were underachieving; they were not picking up the accreditations which were understood to improve their life chances. Hence research and investigation examined the relationship between education and other social processes and focused on what it was specifically in education that should be changed to ameliorate this persistent inequality.[4]

It is possible to examine at least three areas, each of which can bring evidence of inequality in education. The particular emphasis in this chapter will be on gender inequalities.

Achievement

There still persists a 'commonsense' belief that achievement indicates some inner truth about a person's abilities. However, achievement is not natural; its criteria have a conventional base. This is highlighted, for example, by the ways in which such criteria may be the subject of disputes between teachers and examination bodies, during consultation periods. It is important to understand and keep in mind an individual's achievement as the extent to which she or he has taken up the conventions which operate in schools.

Achievement is also competitive. Awards are distributed proportionately. In popular parlance we talk of the top 20 or even ten per cent and the bottom 40%. Achievement is popularly understood as 'doing better than. . .' Schools are now expected to compete on the basis of their achievements. Competitively-based achievement is likely to favour that sex which is more socialised into competition.

It is also the case that what counts as achievement, or what has greater currency, is historical; it changes over time. It now seems the case that 'technological achievement', as so often orchestrated through the 'needs of industry' and 'equipped for life in the 21st century' educational rhetorics, has become central to the purposes of schools, affecting how we are to understand, assess and 'measure' achievements across the entire 'subject-matter' of schooling. This has been a shift in the educational terrain over some years, which has reached profound and specific articulation in the Education Reform Act.

The social construction, values attached and competitiveness of achievement have had negative effects upon girls.[5] Gender difference positions boys and girls differently. Girls are high achievers, but are not always perceived as such, due to their lesser achievements in those areas which have been associated with 'a rational body of knowledge' and higher level of abstraction.[6] Girls' abilities and achievements are linked to aspects of knowledge which are taken to entail lower levels of abstraction and therefore, as it is thought, require a less demanding process of initiation, the 'soft options!'. This intimate connection between achievement and the differential value placed on types of knowledge and modes of thought has been significant in the perception of girls as underachievers. We now need to consider this.

Knowledge

The selection of what constitutes school knowledge has not only a historical and philosophical base, but also a social, cultural and political one. School knowledge has been an area of contention. Debates have taken place over what the curriculum excludes from its subject matter and where it ranks that subject matter in an evaluative hierarchy. These have profound social consequences.

Certain subjects are accorded 'higher' and 'different types' of value. The mathematical and scientifically-based areas of knowledge, involving 'rationality' and high levels of abstraction have historically been construed as relevant to what we might term the 'public' sphere.[7] They have also been socially constructed as masculine and, as previously suggested, 'more difficult'.[8] Subjects which involve more personal, social, communicative

49

and affective modes of thought are construed as more relevant to the 'private' sphere and gendered as feminine. A higher value has been placed on the 'public' sphere; historically and socially girls have been generally absented from it. It should be noted here, that while the National Curriculum compels girls into science and technology, hence removing the inequality of their conspicuous absence, it does not alter anything else in terms of the gendered style of these subjects or indeed of the curriculum as a whole.

The way in which power and knowledge in relation to gender difference affect the curriculum, is also shown in what counts as learning. It is to this that we now turn.

Learning

What constitutes learning is something which is often debated. But when learning is debated, it is not always recognised that learning can be many things. Our society appears to value 'lone intellectual' learning at its 'highest' levels and notions of 'authority' and 'expertise' predominate. In earlier years we may be prepared to accept that learning and playing can be the same thing. It is important to ask whether our view of learning is unequally gendered. We should not be surprised if this is the case. Thus it may be that learning which is seen as collaborative, negotiated and engaging personal perspectives, is not seen as high status. It may be that women are more prepared for this style of learning.[9]

Girls are not socialised as 'autonomous, enquiring beings,' in the way that boys are. Indeed, they are socialised into nurturing these qualities in boys and men, rather than displaying them themselves. Hence, boys' and girls' learning behaviours are likely to be different and boys are more likely to be judged as actual or potential 'real learners', than are girls.[10] This consequence is particularly evident in mixed settings, but also has effects in single-sex settings.

Given the context outlined above, the role of schools can now be considered, both in terms of what has been attempted and what has been achieved.

What can schools do?

Schools have thought about the ways in which forms of achievement, the organisation and content of subject matter and approaches to learning, contribute to inequality. Many schools have developed equal opportunities policies which have sought to build in an awareness that:

- racism, sexism and other forms of oppression are pervasive and insidious and, as schools are not 'separate' from society, they occur in school;
- racial and sexual harassment are manifested in varying forms and they should be recognised and dealt with as such, by all teachers;
- there is likely to be unwitting discriminatory judgement and stereotyping of abilities along race and gender lines;
- the school curriculum, in its processes of selection, differentiation and hierarchisation, helps to produce inequalities;
- the school curriculum marginalises and undervalues certain languages, racial and gender experience and knowledge. It may, indeed, represent the presence of these as a 'problem'.

In the light of these awarenesses, schools have tried to:

- change the curriculum to give greater representation and value to black and female experience;
- make the historical, social, political and economic reasons for sexism, the construction of sexuality and racism, an integral part of the curriculum;
- organise option schemes to alleviate the under-representation of girls in certain subjects and adhere to equality curriculum principles;
- remove or minimise the masculine bias in the logic, representation and perception of certain learning experiences;
- intervene at the level of the classroom and find ways of empowering oppressed groups.

Much change in the area of equal opportunities has been piecemeal. There are good reasons for this.

1 Not all teachers will share the same analysis, particularly of areas of the curriculum, which, on the face of it, seem to offer 'neutrality' of content and learning methods.
.2 Some may perceive the curriculum and its constituents, including teaching and learning practices, as incorporating equal treatment and therefore equality of opportunity.
3 Some teachers may recognise the constraints upon schooling in terms of examinations and assessment, programmes of study and subject matter and in the light of this, view equal opportunity goals as further constraints, impossible tasks or unrealisable, given the time at their disposal.
4 Some may accept equal opportunity goals, but locate the 'roots of the problem' elsewhere and see school as a relatively powerless agent of change.

These views have some degree of credence and cannot simply be dismissed. What is possible, how and in what time-scale, depends on the particular school, its history and its image. This is not to conclude that a) nothing is possible, or b) short-term, piecemeal or limited change is without effect.

Schools and other social processes

In considering the changes which schools can make, it is important to be aware of the limits which may come from 'outside' the institution. Schools which aim to develop an extended state of equality, 'within their own walls' can recognise the inequality existing in the labour market outside, and how the 'reality' of their futures might be perceived by pupils.

Schools may seek to address this through the curriculum and learning within it. However, beyond school, opportunities and the distribution of opportunities are variable and far from equal across gender, race, and class. For working-class girls, confinement to domesticity and the reserve-army of labour, or the lowest paid servicing or caring jobs, is powerfully in play, as too is the depression of opportunity for girls to reach higher economic status in the professional sphere. Given this pressing 'reality' for girl pupils, schools cannot expect the transfer of such learning to be easy or the school's aspirations for its pupils to be simply realised.[11]

Girls' and boys' gendered positions are constantly being shaped and re-shaped by a complex set of familial, other institutional and cultural reproductive practices, apart from those of schooling.[12] School cannot 'over-determine' all these. Attempts to do so, by making assumptions about the 'fixity' of gender and cultural positions, not recognising the complexity, movement across and resistance to these, can be counter-productive.[13]

The point of all this

Having developed a frame of reference and analysis of schools and equal opportunities, we can now consider what purpose it may serve.

One of the problems associated with trying to implement change in relation to equal opportunities, is that there is no clear and coherent programme for change. This may feel disempowering. Efforts in one area may increase frustration at the persistent difficulties in other areas. In making this analysis, reasons for the uneven nature of change have been suggested. A focus on equal opportunities has to include a recognition of the likelihood of piecemeal and uneven development, given the complexity of 'accommodating' and 'resistant' forces present in any one institution. This should not be dispiriting, but can hopefully provide a greater confidence in changes that are taking place, however 'limited' they may seem.

Indeed, time taken to address areas in which inequalities exist can
profitable, if it brings attention to the importance of well-thought-ou
Further, time taken to examine the relationship between schools an
social processes, inside and outside the institution, can be profitable.
help highlight the processes that need to be dealt with and again, develop
realistic goals in that light.

Gender and learning processes in the classroom

Before examining possible change in the classroom, it is useful to consider,
in general terms, the processes of teaching and learning that take place
within it, and how these processes may operate differently for girls and
boys. This involves considering how some of the gender implications in
achievement, knowledge and learning are 'played out' in the classroom.

The classroom is a socially interactive environment, organised through
the learning and subject-matter 'rules' and social 'rules'. These sets of rules
overlap. Although the teacher cannot determine all the effects on pupils of
different kinds or 'levels' of learning or the patterns of social interaction in
the classroom, she or he makes judgements on those and their significance
for ability and achievement. Teachers are continually making evaluative
judgements on pupils' abilities, motivation and behaviour in the classroom.
The teacher's expectations of the learning process involve all these. Given
what we have said about gender and learning, we should not be surprised to
find 'gendered effects' on teachers' expectations.

Boys, as previously suggested, are socialised into more competitive, autonomous and actively-enquiring approaches to learning. These are valued
in schools. Because of the nature of schools and classrooms, learning is a
profoundly public activity and boys are 'gendered' to take the public space,
whereas girls are 'gendered' towards the private sphere.

In classrooms, boys have a greater public presence and are much more
inclined to 'by-pass the rules', both of classroom procedures and subject
matter. Girls are generally more painstaking, with a stricter adherence to
the rules of the subject matter and process.[14]

The more 'authoritative' and challenging characteristics of boys' learning
behaviours, despite the potentially negative effects of their social behaviour,
may be interpreted as demonstrating a greater control over the subject
matter, 'brilliance' and real learning. In contrast, girls' learning behaviours,
in their adherence to the rules, and greater 'privacy' of their actions, may
suggest greater dependency on those rules and passivity.

Given all the factors outlined so far, in relation to achievement, knowledge, learning and their effect in classrooms, girls find themselves having

to negotiate an already 'masculine' terrain. Girls' behaviours are rational strategies for negotiating this terrain, given the context of 'masculine' power and authority in which they find themselves. Being on this terrain of masculine power is a risky business, involving considerable threat to their gendered position. In such a situation, keeping quiet and avoiding the 'public sphere' may make more sense.

Girls may take up other positions which seem empowering for them, by adopting the authority role of the 'teacher/mother'. Or they may adopt the caring role, being helpful and nice, or even turn the classroom into a much more private space of their own friends. All these positions involve both gain and loss. Confining to the private or 'domesticating' the situation are gains, which reinforce the 'feminine' and reaffirm the loss of that 'other' sphere of public power. Publicly challenging the knowledge and being 'brilliant', rather than being insignificant, risks the loss of the 'feminine'. So too, does challenging the teacher and failing to be conformist, which results in being forced back into the 'feminine'.

Thus girls are involved in a difficult balancing act, between public 'brilliance' and conformity. This balancing act may be less difficult and switching positions may be easier if a girl's social class position holds a greater investment in public knowledge. That is, if she is middle class. It may be even more difficult if learning behaviour is also racially defined across the feminine and Afro-Caribbean girls are seen as too non-conformist, Asian girls as too conformist.[15]

Boys do not have to negotiate the masculinity of the terrain. There is less conflict between the 'active, public power' space of learning and their gendered position, although there may be conflicts within the power space of the social and the 'social rules' of the classroom. They may, too, have to perform balancing acts across class and race positions. School definitions of authority, autonomy and the importance of displacing conflict through rational processes, may conflict with their own 'family' generated definitions and processes.

Boys' gendered positions are more likely to involve vying for 'the power', rather than finding alternative forms of empowerment, which seem to characterise girls' strategies. It is not surprising, therefore, that more boys than girls seem to challenge the very 'control' mechanisms of schooling and are represented in much higher numbers in exclusion, suspension and behavioural unit statistics.[16]

The argument presented here is that learning processes as they are 'enacted' in classrooms can have differing social and 'psychological' effects for girls and boys. These effects are bound up with those of the other institutional factors, previously outlined. However, boys' and girls' positions are not necessarily 'forever fixed' positions; the extent to which the inequality in these effects is *confirmed* and *realised* in the classroom, is open to change. It now remains to consider how change can be brought about in the classroom.

There is a feeling (understandable, given the complex structures schools are and given the classroom's relationship to all those constraints and factors that interplay in 'getting through the business of teaching and learning') that the classroom is likely to be the least amenable site for change, or that what a teacher and a class can put into effect is going to be made negligible by the mass of forces outside the classroom.

However, looked at in another way, classrooms are environments that can be changed in any number of ways, from layout, display, equipment, activities occuring in them, to the forms of interaction that take place in them. Classrooms are also situations that in some ways can be changed more rapidly than other structures and systems in a school.[17]

Many teachers are aware that unless things begin to happen at the level of the classroom, much initiative and concern for equal opportunity will 'fail to connect'. Thus the classroom is a key site, although a complex one. To 'simplify away' this complexity is not helpful, rather it needs to be brought to the fore, clarified and put into context, so that elements within it can be perceived as open to change, even in the 'smallest' ways. It is disempowering to expect too much from classrooms or to assume that 'disembodied exhortations' about equal opportunities can be miraculously transformed into real change by teachers, but steps can be taken, experiments performed and a few moves made. It now remains to consider these.

Change in the classroom

Classrooms are environments which carry and produce social messages. These social messages interact with and help to produce and sustain learning behaviours. In this case, we are interested in those gendered social messages.

We tend to think that behaviour is something students bring with them into the classroom which teachers to a greater or lesser extent have to control. The problem with this is that it may suggest that the classroom is a neutral environment, a kind of backdrop or stage for behaviours formed elsewhere; and it tends to focus on behaviour as something 'inside' the individual rather than shaped by a number of influences and effects, many of which are attributable to the design of interaction in the classroom.[18]

As previously outlined, boys and girls will enter the classroom with differing predispositions towards learning and the learning environment. The question is, what factors do we need to look at when considering how far the classroom can sustain or reduce the inequality of opportunity that gender differences in learning behaviour may imply? These can be looked at in terms of 'environment design' factors, such as layout of the room, display and the design of tasks and 'interactive design' factors, such as time, movement, teacher-pupil interaction and pupil-pupil interaction.

Environment factors

Layout

The layout of the room marks the 'original' space of the room and can also carry messages as to the kind of learning behaviour expected in it. Rows of individual desks or groups of tables probably provide the most evocative distinction. A room may also be marked by particular areas for particular activities or uses, signified by equipment or resources. Some rooms may be particularly marked and more 'static' in their arrangements than others, such as science laboratories or design workshops for specific practical purposes.

In general terms a room can signify more individualised and private activities (although classrooms are always public places) or more demonstrative ones, more dependence on teacher instruction, or less.

Boys and girls will tend to occupy these spaces differently. Boys tend to generate a greater presence anyway, whatever the layout, through their body language, their way of moving into seats, the spread of their belongings and their leaning back on chairs. Girls tend to generate more 'enclosed' occupancy. They may build on this by seeking out more peripheral or enclosing spaces in the room and define quite specific sub-groups.

From observations, this is particularly apparent in larger, specifically orientated rooms, like science labs, where girls have been observed sitting in the most peripheral locations, or close to the teacher, but in fact under her line of vision and away from the action.[19] In fact it has been noted that whenever there is an actual or possible 'centre stage' or 'centre of attention' in a classroom, it is more likely to be occupied by boys. Particular areas of a classroom may become 'marked' as boys' or girls' areas, according to what equipment is placed there, where the door and windows are etc.

While these distribution patterns are not going to be exactly the same in every classroom, nearly all classroom layouts become more or less 'gender marked' and this has consequences for boys' and girls' learning. Where people sit may not be as arbitrary as we may think; it can be affect the amount and quality of attention they receive and re-inforce particular levels of confidence or dominance.

What can be done about layout?

1 First, it is useful to draw a plan of the classroom and plot how the space is or can be occupied, including what marks the teacher's space and the orientation of teaching from it.

2 Think about this classroom space in relation to gender.
3 If the corners or edges appear to be gendered zones, try removing them by creating a semi-circular space.
4 If particular equipment areas tend to be occupied by girls or boys in ways which are reinforcing differential and unequal learning experience, try moving the equipment areas, or changing the orientation of the room around them.
5 In particularly 'fixed' environments, like labs and workshops, where the layout cannot easily be changed, consider how the teacher's usual 'marked position' determines the learning space and the effects of changing that.

Display
Having considered students' possible interactions with the layout of the room, it is also important to consider display. Display is another vehicle for social messages about the kind of activities and purpose expected of a room and whom that room is addressing. Girls and boys may well react to this differently.

A great deal of concern around display has focused, quite rightly, on the content of images and how far they reflect positive images of a multicultural and over half female British society. There has been considerable impetus in producing images of women in science and technology, for example. This is all to the good and it is extremely important that the school environment positively identify black people and women as legitimate constituents, through its displays.

In more general ways, there are also questions of what display may signify in terms of the 'style' of the classroom and the learning that takes place within it. Style can carry 'gendered' meanings. There is a sense in which we can say an environment or even an object appears 'masculine' or 'feminine'.

We usually make such distinctions along the following lines:

- *Masculine* – darker/neutral colour, smooth/hard texture, hard-edged, abstract, larger-scale, bold.
- *Feminine* – lighter/brighter colour, softer texture, soft-edged, detailed, smaller-scale, intricate and intimate.[20]

These are historical and cultural determinations, indeed, Western determinations. When we are talking about the 'ethos' of rooms and the more intangible messages they convey, such considerations do have a place. It is possible that a preponderance of hard-edged, 'flat', abstract imagery in rather 'de-textured' 'neutral' settings, mechanistic in ethos, can be inhibiting to girls. It is also possible that if such an ethos is additionally marked by notices couched in 'do not' terms, the environment can seem prohibitive to girls.[21]

What can be done about display?
There are certain elements in a room's appearance that teachers cannot change. The extent to which any one teacher can hold a degree of 'ownership' of a room depends on individual circumstances. Nevertheless, signs of attention to the environment by the teacher have an important effect on students' expectations of that environment and some attention to 'gender appeal' can significantly influence student perceptions of a 'subject-matter' and how far that subject matter is 'for them'.

1 It is important to regularly examine and change display.
2 Consider what kind of ethos and 'image' of a subject is being generated by the display characteristics of the room.
3 Change and vary colours of notices and their styles of address.
4 Soften predominantly hard, abstract characteristics by adding varieties of texture, colour, tone and detail.
5 Consider ways of making 'mechanistic image' rooms more 'people-centred' and affective through display.

Tasks or activities

The tasks or activities students are to engage in are environment factors, although they also bear considerably on interactive factors. What is at issue here is the effect different tasks have on the 'feel' of the learning environment for boys and girls and how this affects their approach to learning.

In general terms, some tasks are more public than others. Some tasks are more autonomous than others. Autonomy relates to the degree of 'self-direction' in a task. Public relates to the extent to which a task is 'visible' and open to scrutiny. Obviously different tasks require different skills, or a different combination of skills and different uses of the class environment. There are likely to be gender differences in preference for, confidence in, and general appeal of, different tasks.

Girls are more likely than boys to prefer and have confidence in less public activities, like personal reading and writing. They may, however, feel more open to scrutiny than boys when these activities are made public. Girls are more likely than boys to appreciate writing as a developmental task, involving drafting processes; boys have a greater tendency to avoid such processes and feel that they have no use for them. There are factors involving 'security' in writing for girls, which pertain less to boys. 'Safety' in writing will not necessarily signify autonomy in learning to teachers.

Tasks involving the use of equipment can often develop into boy-dominated activities. Boys will tend to approach the use of equipment with much more 'bravado' than girls, will monopolise it and improvise with it, extending its use and its effect on the classroom environment. In mixed groups boys can often be seen 'at the controls' of the equipment and in boys' groups equipment is played around with and turned to other uses.

58

Paradoxically, this does not always mean boys will fail to achieve the results intended from the equipment's use. Their greater confidence with equipment and 'rougher and readier' approach can enable them to use equipment more effectively in undaunted ways and certainly achieve faster results. Equipment-centred tasks also have a greater publicness about them which can add to girls' inhibition. Thus, although boys may be less compliant in equipment's prescribed uses, their approach may suggest greater autonomy as learners to teachers.[22]

Some tasks involve students working together and adopting work roles within a group. In mixed groupings, girls will tend to occupy the 'maintenance' roles and boys the 'directive' roles (there is also the 'unofficial' saboteur role, which tends to be taken by a boy!). Decision-making will tend to be taken over by the boys, while girls will attempt to keep to the necessary procedures of the task. Girls are more likely to keep the group 'on task', by maintaining the group process and servicing the situation, but this does not afford them *power* in the process and its outcomes.

These are just some aspects of tasks which indicate that they are not neutral contributors to the classroom environment and its gender interaction patterns. Clearly, subject-matter and the processes associated with particular subjects seem to determine the 'inevitability' of certain tasks, so can anything be done?

What can be done about tasks?

1 Variety. It is not unusual for one activity to occupy a lesson with no change of 'learning style' required. If lack of variety is repeated from lesson to lesson, students soon build up fixed notions of a subject matter and patterns of behaviour that go with it, which can entrench gender perceptions. Hence it is important to vary activities.

2 Timing and change of pace. Teachers may set the timing of activities at the beginning of a lesson, without building in planned interventions to change the time and pace of tasks. This can have gendered effects. While girls may conscientiously go through the stages, with greater or lesser confidence, depending on the activity, boys may take short cuts to create time for themselves.

3 Unplanned or insufficiently communicated time-scales for tasks tend to increase gender differences in behaviour and the dominance of the environment by boys. Thus the teacher needs to plan stages with gender in mind and clearly communicate each step, its time and pace, beforehand and in the course of a lesson.

4 Balancing tasks between genders. If decisions regarding 'who does what' in group situations, (especially mixed ones) are generally left to the pupils, the likelihood of inequalities in power over the group events is increased. It is important both to monitor the power dimensions and to redress unequal balances. This involves:

- clearly communicating the goals of the task and its working demands;
- clearly explaining the nature of the student collaboration and giving guidelines on group roles;
- allocating a specific role to each pupil in the group;
- allocating more powerful roles to girls and intervening on turn-taking, where there is evidence of male dominance;
- nominating one or two pupils to monitor who does what in groups and discussing the power dimensions of groups with pupils;

5 Predicting and controlling the use of equipment. If equipment tends to be merely put at students' disposal there are fairly predictable outcomes in terms of gender. Boys will dominate its use and 'masculinise' its purposes. This can be alleviated through:

- predicting the likely gender effects of the introduction of items of equipment into learning tasks;
- preparation, to avoid some of the more obvious ones;
- control of the distribution and redistribution of equipment in the course of a lesson;
- time and use allocations being made clear beforehand;
- girls being given specific opportunities to control the equipment.

* * * * *

These are some of the environment factors that teachers can attend to and change. The next stage is to consider those classroom interactive factors. Teachers may feel more tightly enmeshed in these and hence they may seem even more difficult to identify and/or deal with.

Interactive factors

Interaction in a classroom is varied, continual, dispersed and simultaneous. To open it to systematic analysis and thus possible change, some identifying categories may help. We can distinguish 'interactive modes' in terms of time; movement; talk; teacher-pupil interaction; pupil-pupil interaction.*

Time
We have touched on some issues relating to time when considering some task factors. The focus here is on time as an interactive factor. What do boys and girls do with time in the classroom? What purposes does it serve them? How might it be perceived by the teacher?

---

*   These are the five themes of classroom rules identified by Hargreaves DH et al (1975) *Deviance in Classrooms*, Routledge and Kegan Paul

Boys create time for themselves by working at speed with less attention to detail and the controls of the task. Creating time for themselves facilitates their dominance of the space and enables wider interaction patterns across the classroom. At times, it may give them the competitive kudos of 'finishing first'. Boys' use of time generally gives them a greater sense of their control and autonomy in the learning situation, as opposed to their perception of girls' dependence on the time set. This can be reinforced by teachers' interpretations of their approach to time as independence, control and 'brilliance'.

Girls' approach to time appears to be more continuous, less digressive and more to do with evenness of pace and reliance on the predictability of events, than the creation of 'new ones'. Girls may invest more in deliberation over tasks. This does not mean that they do not make the time their own in classroom situations, but their divergent uses of time are less extrovert and evident and are less about dominating the environment.

Girls' and boys' uses of and responses to time are part of the simultaneity of classroom events. Teachers attend to numerous aspects of classroom life at the same time. In this sense, while teachers may have planned time objectives, they have to negotiate time and its uses in lessons. Teachers more or less predict the time and pace of tasks and, in the course of lessons, are concerned with 'getting things done'.

Certain factors enter into their predictions of time and pace of tasks and their reworking of time in the course of lessons.[23] These include choosing which 'events' to ignore and which to attend to in a lesson; pacing the timing of questions, waiting time and timing of response; judging which deliberations, explorations or reflections are salient to the lesson and which are not. Some activities may require greater pupil autonomy in terms of pupils determining their own time structures.

This may mean that teachers' negotiations of time in lessons are influenced more by boys' uses of time than girls' uses. In addition, the perceived use of time by boys makes responsive demands on teachers to give them more attention and re-assert 'teacher control' of time, intervene as facilitators/ controllers more with boys, extend, deliver more or change tasks or sometimes even re-order lesson priorities.[24] The greater speed of boys' responses to questions and their greater autonomy in using time, may be perceived as an advantage in getting things done. If girls' use of time is less demanding, it may function less as a negotiable feature in lessons. Further, under the pressure and 'shape' of getting things done, 'girls' time' and more deliberative and tentative modes of thought may be cut short.

Managing time
A teacher has to be a skilful manager of time. This management has to be understood in relation to planning activities and establishing routines which, in relation to gender, seek to reduce, in the first instance, ambiguities in time use. The most important factors would seem to be:

- establishing routines prior to the commencement of tasks, to do with seating arrangements, pens, paper, other equipment, etc;
- clearly stating 'time goals' for tasks and the reasons for them and building time appraisals into the lesson;
- establishing routines for change-overs from one task to another and giving clear prior indication of change-over times;
- establishing routines for pupils checking their work.

Further strategies could then focus on the unequalising effects of time use between girls and boys:

- being clear about the purposes of time in relation to activities; structuring them so that time is allowed and expected for attention to detail, thinking and reflection, as part of the process;
- building in a range of times within/across activities, which do not qualitatively 'favour' speed in execution;
- being attentive to the time emphases in the structuring of questions and answers, for example, so that the instant question/ instant response is not always the major emphasis and the most recognised;
- providing opportunities for girls to use independence and directive skills in the timing of activities.

Movement

Boys move more than girls. It appears to be a gendered characteristic of body language that boys spread their limbs, lean back, stretch out and generally stand and sit with the effect of occupying more space. They also spread their belongings more, so move more to get things. They move around the classroom much more than girls. They move more quickly into classrooms, into spaces, towards equipment than girls. They are more competitive about occupying space. They have a greater tendency to ignore others' occupation of space, by moving through, encroaching on or leaning over others' spaces in classrooms.[25]

The effect of all this is that boys physically assert themselves much more than girls and 'make their presence felt' in particularly active ways, which exert more control over and dominance of the classroom environment and the girls within it.

Movement in the classroom can be seen as interfering with the learning process, or it may be a greater or lesser constituent part of it, or it may signify active, enthusiastic engagement, depending on the context. Teachers have to make the parameters and purposes for movement clear and manage them in the course of lessons. This can be complex, given that movement can serve different purposes at the same time for pupils; moving to get equipment, for example, can also involve quite extensive social interaction. Thus teachers cannot always accurately predict movement and its effects on the classroom environment and its social consequences.

It is important to recognise the relationship between movement and power and confidence within the environment, emphasised by the publicness of schools and classrooms. Girls have to negotiate these power dimensions every day, in corridors, in playgrounds and in classrooms. It is not surprising that many develop alternative strategies and find or create 'safe' locations, rather than enter this public arena.[26]

What can be done about movement?

1 First consider the social messages in movement and monitor their use and effects in classrooms. This will give a clearer picture of its social dynamic, beyond its interpretation as liveliness, active engagement and (over)enthusiasm, with its implied opposites of passivity and lack of confidence in learning.
2 When planning activities, predict some likely movement outcomes in the context of what the activity is, where it will take place, where the equipment will be placed, the timing and the kind of task change overs that will occur. (They will not all be predictable, but a lot will!)
3 Organise the task environment to more closely structure and circumscribe the necessary movement.
4 Order and stage movement around the room to reduce numbers moving at any one time; be precise about its direction and purposes.
5 Allocate the tasks involving movement or roles in activities to specific pupils and avoid always responding to and reinforcing the 'wanderers'.

Talk

Talk is probably understood as a key interactive process in classrooms and indeed it is difficult to consider talk apart from teacher-pupil, pupil-pupil interrelations. However a few comments about its qualities in relation to gender and how it operates as a process in classrooms will be useful.

Contrary to some popular myths, boys talk more than girls. In addition, studies indicate that boys' actual utterances tend to be shorter than girls', while they occur more often with fewer pauses. Boys' talk is more 'product' and information-oriented. It is more inclined to be directive, as opposed to girls' talk which is more extensive in utterance, but contains more pauses and cues to the listener and is generally more oriented towards attitudes, feelings and 'social dimensions'.[27]

Teacher talk in classrooms is goal-directed and task-related; is public and authority laden. It varies between being elaborative (with pauses to 'check' the listener) and usually direct questioning. A considerable amount of teacher talk is instructional. This establishes the context for classroom talk, so that the more personal exchanges and the 'socialising' dimensions of talk, which are present in the classroom, are set in this context.

This presents a prevailing climate for talk which may be more suited to boys than girls. Given classroom talk's directedness to goals and tasks, it implies for students quick responses, assertion in establishing the framework for exchanges that moves the task on, direction rather than reflection, selectivity, rather than repetition and redundancy, and – in general – a mode of talking which keeps 'tight control' over the linguistic space. This may be further emphasised if teachers tend to direct shorter utterances to boys, confirming the kind of talk that is predominantly in play.

Talk structures and learning
While this mode of talking is characterised by efficiency, there are questions about its effectiveness as a mode of learning. Research suggests that talk is more effective as a learning device if people are given the time and space to collect thoughts and speak, if the emphasis is on explanation and processes, rather than end results, if it is co-operative and adaptive to response rather than closed.[28]

It would seem important both for educational goals and gender relations within them to balance talk processes in classrooms, so that quick response, assertion, and tightly-controlled utterance do not always predominate amongst pupils.

This predominance may appear more evident in settings which emphasise whole class 'instruction' and public recitation of question and answer, but it can also characterise smaller-group settings.[29]

Thus it is important that teachers:

- monitor talk processes in the classroom's different settings;
- provide opportunities for different talk climates in lessons;
- intervene to encourage and structure more co-operative and open group talk patterns;
- develop students' awareness of talk processes through specific talk tasks.

These are issues which necessarily relate to teacher-pupil and pupil-pupil interactions and talk will obviously come into these contexts.

Teacher-pupil interaction
A considerable amount of research has been conducted on teacher-pupil interactions in relation to gender, with substantial agreement on results. Teachers interact significantly more with boys than with girls. It has been demonstrated many times over that in mixed classrooms boys receive some 70% or more of teacher attention.[30] This is, of course, a generalisation from numerous studies and across different settings; important qualifications may have to be made about how many boys (there are some less-demanding ones!) and what kinds of attention. However, lots of teachers in mixed schools are aware of the disproportionate amount of attention they give to boys and are concerned about it.

64

What concerns them most is boys' behaviour and the demands it makes on them to control it.[31] Thus they may see their interactions with boys primarily as forms of 'discipline contacts'. This needs to be looked at carefully, as it is evident that teachers' interactions with boys, disproportionate as they are, compared to those with girls are certainly not all overtly 'disciplinary' and negative.[32]

Significantly, some research has suggested that teachers' interactions with black boys, especially those deemed to be 'low achievers' are more negative than those with white boys.[33] Other studies on girls suggest that when girls are younger, they initiate more contacts with teachers than boys, to seek teacher approval. As girls get older, this 'seeking approval' contact diminishes. This reduction in initiating contact occurs earlier for black girls than for white girls, with the suggestion that black girls more quickly fail to achieve positive results from these contacts.[34]

This is not to suggest that individual teachers are, as a rule, loaded with stereotypical assumptions about black pupils' behaviours and achievements, but that there may be a gap between teachers' positions in, and understandings of, learning situations and black pupils' understandings of them. These race-gender dimensions are critical and should not be overlooked, or undermined when looking at inequalities in classrooms.

With such qualifications in mind, it can be said that teachers:[35]

- direct more questions to boys than to girls;
- respond to boys' hand-raising, calling out or interrupting to answer more than to girls';
- give boys more feedback in terms of prompting, clarifying, elaborating on their answers or comments;
- direct closed questions to girls and give less expansive forms of feedback;
- initiate more interactions with boys than girls and respond to the greater number of pupil-initiated interactions which come from boys;
- give more procedural and process help to boys;
- give less behaviour criticism to girls, but are more likely to criticise girls for academic performance and incorrect answers;
- reprimand boys and girls in different ways, tending to give 'harder', more aggressive, but shorter verbalisations to boys and more 'appealing' but often longer ones to girls.

These teacher-pupil relations, as we have said, are interactive and kept in play by all parties. Teachers' interactions are as much context-dependent and reactive as they are instrumental in forming the context.

It is an explanation to suggest that teachers are pressed into responding to certain forms of behaviour that interfere with learning. It may not be a full explanation. Only some kinds of teacher attention are recognisably related to conduct, which is not to deny that other types of interaction, not ostensibly connected with behaviour, may serve as preventative and 'maintenance of control' measures.

Considering how boys interact with the classroom environment; where they position themselves, how they use time, movement, their approach to tasks and their preference for 'doing', 'making', 'manipulating' activities, a great deal of teacher attention may be taken up with getting boys to observe the procedures of tasks.[36] This is time consuming, although it may not be seen to be teacher behaviour in the same negative category as dealing with disruption.

Another dimension is that boys can be perceived to be more active participants as learners, demonstrating qualities which are valued in learning contexts, such as confidence in asking questions and quick response, a sense of challenge, assertion in public situations and a sense of public achievement.[37]

Boys have fewer qualms about answering questions directed to them, calling out answers to generally-directed questions, chipping in on class discussions, volunteering for (the higher status) tasks, asking questions and seeking clarification. In doing these things they interrupt others and claim 'speaking rights', steer class discussions in directions of most interest to them, circumvent classroom procedures and learning procedures, and take the public space. These gendered positions signify power in the classroom.[38]

Girls, as we have seen, have to negotiate this power in the classroom, from their own gendered positions, at considerable risk. Their gendered learning behaviours are not about public assertion, public display or challenge. Girls are not gendered into *competing* for the right to answer, the right to speak, the right to the public space, the right to individualistic achievement. To enter the domain of 'masculine'-dominated learning involves the threat, in the first place, of masculine derision, which accompanies male competitiveness and also a 'violation' of their 'femininity'.

Thus girls' different approach and response to learning is less likely to involve behaviours which, for a variety of reasons, draw attention from others.

When it does, and girls are reprimanded, this may take forms which suggest that teachers have different expectations of girls than of boys. These reinscribe girls in the 'feminine' and further the vulnerability of their status and reputation.[39]

In respect of what the different interaction patterns of boys and girls keep in play, teachers may:

- direct more questions to boys to keep them interested or because they seem more interested;
- respond to boys' indications to answer and call-outs because boys are more urgent and persistent, as they are highly competitive; this urgency

of response can be seen as 'keeping things going' and moving the subject matter along and as 'bright' responses;

- give more elaborate feedback to boys because boys enter into the public arena of question and answer with more confidence and seem to 're-spond' to it more positively or because their behaviour suggests they need more elaborate feedback;
- direct more closed questions to girls, because *publicly* girls may be seen as dealing less successfully with more open-ended questions;
- initiate more interaction with boys and respond to boys' initiation of contact because they need to maintain and gear their interest, or be-cause teachers perceive a more active engagement from boys; and be-cause boys' requests are more demanding in their mode;
- direct more procedural interaction to boys, because girls are seen to 'just get on with it';
- direct more academic than behaviour criticism to girls, because relative to behaviour or appearance of work, that is going to have a higher profile for teachers with regards to girls;
- reprimand boys and girls differently because their differing behaviours and 'attitudes' towards 'rule breaking' seem to beg different modes of response.[40]

Given these dimensions, it is not surprising that boys receive so much more attention and classrooms can be seen to advantage boys. It is important to recognise that teachers do not directly *cause* this unequal distribution of power in classrooms. If this were so then once teachers were aware of it they could alter the situation much more easily than they can in fact do.[41] Teachers, because of the nature of teaching, learning and classrooms and the gender predispositions within them, interact with this power dynamic and by those interactions can reinforce it, to a greater or lesser extent.

It is the lesser extent that we need to focus on. We need to find ways of interacting with pupils which can begin to reduce this unequal power. Some suggestions follow.

1 The first way to be conscious of gender difference in teacher-pupil interaction is to monitor it. Self-monitoring is difficult, although not impossible. For best results, it probably requires the support of col-leagues, willing to share monitoring each other's lessons. It is also worth involving pupils in monitoring how the class interacts with the teacher as a basis for discussion of the issues with them.

2 Try to avoid using extensive 'whole class' teaching, which emphasises the publicness of the classroom, and encourages 'individualistic' approaches to learning, competitiveness and boys impressing each other with public performances. (However, the alternative, usually described as 'small group' teaching, will not eradicate gender differences in

demands on teachers, although the demands may be of a different nature. This will be discussed under pupil-pupil interaction.)

3   Establish a routine for the answering of questions, alternating between boys and girls and providing regular, positive and elaborated feedback to girls; having previously established a supportive climate for answering, which is not always begging the quickest and the 'best' answer.

4   Establish and make explicit a procedural code for answering questions; it is hand-up and wait.

5   Formalise the 'rules' for speaking; institute the 'no interruptions' rule and systematic turn taking, and point out when the rules are broken.

6   Use specific formal talk activities, like prepared talks and debate, so that class talk is not always geared towards quick response and sudden public exposure.

7   Organise whole class discussion as 'buzz sessions' with pupils in pairs, having a minute to prepare an answer to a question.[42]

8   Try to be absolutely clear on procedures and timing of tasks, writing them on the board, explaining and re-iterating them beforehand, giving ample warning of transitions.

Pupil-pupil interaction

Many interactions which could be described as teacher-pupil, are closely bound up with those between pupils. Many of the behaviours, situations and events to which teachers respond stem from pupil-pupil interaction.

Boys are noticeably more physical and aggressive in their interactions, particularly with each other but also with girls. Boys' interactions with each other can be highly competitive. They may also be humiliating to girls. Some boys quite persistently humiliate girls by remarking on their physical appearance and their sexuality; referring to their incompetence; generally making them the butt for various jokes and derisions; making simulated sexual advances. A great deal of boys' behaviour towards girls is sexual harrassment, although it is not always recognised as such. Added to this, girls do not often complain; they often act with deference towards the boys or laugh it off. To do otherwise risks further humiliation.[43]

Boys also tend to 'put each other down'. This 'putting down' seems to be part of their competitiveness. Boys seem to be gendered into continually proving their masculinity, according to some quite tightly prescriptive stereotypes and 'rules'.[44] These 'rules' tend to characterise 'maleness' in terms of physical strength and aggression, prowess at sport, and resistance to displays of emotions and feelings. This can lead to particular intolerance of characteristics deemed as 'too feminine', with accompanying oppressive derision of other boys as 'cissy' or 'queer', or the particularly extreme way of demonstrating 'male' attributes of physical power and strength which occurs with bullying.

Apart from such extremes, competitive 'put down' exchanges can be part of many other interactions between boys. Many boys characterise each other by their physical achievements, bravado and possessions rather than more personal or intimate qualities. Impersonality, physicality and competition can characterise boys' working relationships as well. When given group tasks they are much more likely to approach them competitively than are girls. They are more likely to each do their own task, rather than cooperate. Conversation is usually a deviation from the task, rather than a means of organising their way through it. They are more likely to compete for equipment than genuinely share it. Many role play situations performed by boys develop into competitive and more physical scenarios. Studies have shown that when working individually, although boys are more effective in seeking help, they are far less likely to obtain it from other boys, than from girls or teachers.[45]

While boys may have to 'prove' and 'live up to' masculinity among each other they also have to affirm their superiority over girls. As previously suggested, some boys affirm this superiority through various types of humiliation they inflict on girls, which 'control' girls into subordinate positions. They also do so by positioning girls as servicers to their needs, not having the same rights as boys to take the lead and initiate. In classroom interactions, girls will often service boys with equipment, answers to questions, guidance on tasks and attention to their personal needs.[46] In mixed working groups, boys will tend to take the higher-status, directive roles and girls the lower-status, maintenance roles. In mixed-group discussions, boys will utilise discussion as a vehicle for assertion, by interrupting girls and dominating the theme and the linguistic space.[47] They may monopolise and take equipment from girls, as if girls have no right to use it.

It is important to remember that what are in play are gendered characteristics and predispositions rather than 'individual' qualities. Due to different gender factors both boys and girls are caught in a dilemma of gain and loss. Girls are ascribed gender positions of being helpful, supportive, cooperative rule-followers. Thus, it is against the 'gender grain' to compete against boys on boys' terms. Hence girls have a predisposition towards alternative modes of behaviour, which – because of the social power in play – tend to confirm their subordination.[48]

This is not to say that girls are not competitive with each other. They are encouraged to value themselves in terms of their physical appearance, in comparison with other girls/women. Their self-esteem depends on social comparison in this way and this particular pressure can be very strong, with deep ramifications for girls.[49] But the development of self-esteem through competition is not as extensive for girls, as it is for boys[50] nor does it operate across as wide a range of attributes.

Girls are also encouraged to value themselves in complementary roles to others, as helpers and carers, both towards other girls and toward boys. In their working relationships with boys they serve them. In working relationships with other girls they mutually help each other and approach group tasks as co-operative efforts, requiring the collaboration of the skills existing within the group. They are also gendered into using language in more nurturing and organising ways than demanding and controlling ones. Girls will use verbal and listening skills to 'make space' for others and exchange views towards co-operative development of ideas and to shape and organise co-operative tasks.[51]

Girls are also more inclined towards the sharing of personal issues and feelings and are generally more sensitive towards the personal. This does mean that conflict between girls is much more personal conflict than boys' competitive 'impersonalised' conflict over 'masculinity'. As we have seen, boys' sexuality is ascribed across a range of activities and public achievements. Girls' sexuality is much more narrowly ascribed across personal qualities and appearance. Thus a considerable amount of conflict between girls stems from defence of 'reputation'.[52]

What does all this suggest for teachers and their role in relationship to pupils' interactions?

The power dynamic in boys' interactions with each other clearly suggests that they are more receptive than girls to competition and individualism – which are factors of achievement in schools. The extent to which the classroom and a school marks this in its ethos, through individualised achievement and concern with comparison of 'results' and end products between pupils, is likely to advantage boys. However, boys' competitiveness is problematic for teachers, accompanied as it is with less positive attributes for learning. A climate which stresses these factors is also likely to reinforce and stress the other factors that go with it, which undermine successful learning for boys themselves and for girls. In the same way, a classroom ethos which presents 'authority' as power and aggression is likely to confirm those attributes in boys and deny both boys and girls more constructive learning relationships.

One view of education recognises that successful learning and greater equality in its outcomes depends upon creating classroom climates of mutual respect, trust and support, with a stronger sense of collaboration in the learning process. Such a view clearly has to address the marked differences in boys' and girls' interactions with each other and with learning.

Girls are better predisposed towards this kind of climate; boys need to acquire the skills to help establish it and work in it. Paradoxically, teachers may feel they have to continue to attend more to the boys, to support them in acquiring the skills which in the long term will benefit them and the girls.

Another cause for concern is the separation of boys and girls in the classroom. Clearly there are inequality issues relating to where boys and girls place themselves; who takes the dominant space; and the competitive effects of boys working together.

However (and it is an important however) unless there are the conditions for frequent monitoring and very carefully considered intervention and structural support from teachers, mixed grouping appears to disadvantage girls considerably.[53]

Are there ways out of the dilemma?

Recognising the extent of disadvantage to girls in mixed classrooms, some schools and teachers create single-sex groupings for girls. Sometimes this is more of a demographic decision, when boys so outnumber girls in a year group that it is impossible to distribute girls across certain specific subject groupings without vast discrepancies in numbers.

Sometimes it is a subject-based decision. Girls' groups are created to give them the space and teacher-time to enhance their confidence and improve their skills in manipulative and conceptual subjects such as science, maths, design and technology (usually seen as masculine) where girls lack confidence and perform less well.

In some instances girls' groups are created for pastoral/social education. Anti-sexist work is sometimes done specifically with girls, without the male/female power dynamics that would exist in mixed settings.

The advantage with such a strategy is that it achieves what it sets out to do. Girls do improve in confidence, self-esteem and achievement in those subject areas, and begin to challenge stereotypical gender ascriptions, through social education.

At first, in the subject-specific contexts, girls may view the establishing of girls' groups as confirming their lack of abilities and their weakness in coping with boys. This, however, depends on the messages they receive through the approach and expectations teachers have, rather than the strategy itself.[54]

A difficulty in being able to implement the strategy is that it may be seen to be impractical in terms of staffing/timetable organisation etc. Another problem may arise in a context of strong commitment to co-education, where the organisation may not be prepared to countenance this form of positive support for girls.

Despite the difficulties operating in mixed classrooms, it is important to try out ways of developing more co-operative learning situations. The emphasis should be on the design and organisational structure of lessons and tasks within them, rather than on 'controlling' individual personalities.

The following are some approaches which could be used.

1 Structure group work *as* group work, with clearly-assigned, even nominated pupil roles and tasks towards a group goal. This means designing tasks and selecting group roles (particularly for boys) on the basis of what skills they can offer to the group, as a group. Avoid setting tasks which can easily dissolve into groups sitting together but doing their own work.

2 Monitor group work on the basis of who is benefiting and in what ways. This can be discussed with pupils, particularly if you can involve them in monitoring it as well, rather than simply an appraisal of end results.

3 Talk between pupils can also be structured by tasks which specifically require pupils to listen to each other and take turns in speaking. This entails more precision than the usual 'discuss in groups and report back' situation, which boys tend to individualise and compete in. This may require devising various pair-work talk activities, which can then be built upon for group activities.
4 Other activities, where talk is not necessarily the main focus, can be approached in the same way.
5 Various devices and simulations can be incorporated into lessons, whatever their ostensible subject-matter, to enable pupils to concentrate on, practise and strengthen group skills and co-operation between individuals.

What can be concluded?
The suggestions in this chapter for changing the gender dynamics of classrooms have a degree of tentativeness about them. They are suggestions which focus very deliberately on changing and improving the conditions for learning and attempting to make them more equal between boys and girls, through concentrating on the design of interaction in the classroom environment.

Looking precisely at what the gender dynamics are and how they are played out in the classroom as an environment can clarify perspectives on change and keep these closely in the classroom context. Ideas for changing interaction patterns in classrooms cannot offer 'blueprints' for success. Such change requires experiment 'in situ', with, no doubt, many modifications to original plans, depending on the results. It can also be disempowering to overestimate the likely effectiveness of strategies before implementing them.

A positive way forward would be for teachers to become experimental 'action researchers' in their classrooms and see what the outcomes are. This can be helped by a supportive network of teachers, within and across schools, who can share ideas and help each other in trying things out in the classroom. It is hoped that this chapter has stimulated interest in such a proposition.

References

1 For discussion of equal opportunities as an educational issue see: Weiner, G. (1987) 'Equal Opportunities, Feminism and Girls' Education – Introduction' in Weiner, G. (ed), *Just a Bunch of Girls*, Open University Press 'Gender in Education' Series; Arnot, M. and Weiner, G. (1987) 'Teachers and Gender Politics' in Arnot, M. and Weiner, G.

(eds), *Gender and the Politics of Schooling*, Hutchinson/Open University Press.

2   See Amos, V. and Parmar, P. (1987) 'Resistances and and Responses: the experience of Black Girls in Britain' in Arnot, M. and Weiner, G. (eds) *Gender and the Politics of Schools*, Hutchinson/Open University Press.
    Brah, A. and Minhas, R. (1987) 'Structural racism or cultural difference: schooling for Asian girls' in Weiner, G. (ed) *Just a Bunch of Girls*, Open University Press.

3   See Lavigeur, J. (1982) 'Coeducation and the Tradition of Separate Needs', appendix in Sarah, E. and Spender, D. *Learning to Lose*, Womens' Press; and Scott, M. (1982) 'Teach her a lesson: Sexist Curriculum in Patriarchal Education-ideological justifications: official policy and ordinary beliefs' in *Learning to Lose*.

4   See Inner London Education Authority (1981) *Achievement in Schools: sex differences*, Report RS806/81.
    For a critical view of 'equality of opportunity' see Troyna, B. (1987) 'A conceptual overview of strategies to combat racial inequality in education' in Troyna, B. (ed) *Racial Inequality in Education*, Tavistock publications; Williams, J. (1987) 'The construction of women and black students as educational problems: re-evaluating policy on gender and "race"' in *Gender and the Politics of Schooling*.

5   For an investigation into sex differences in achievement-related beliefs and behaviours and how these affect academic choices and attainments, see Licht, B. and Dweck, C. (1987) 'Sex differences in achievement orientations' in Arnot, M. and Weiner, G. (eds) *Gender and the Politics of Schooling*.

6   For a theoretical discussion of the historical privileging of 'rational bodies of knowledge' and its accompanying exclusions and oppressions see Henriques, J., Holloway, W., Urwin, C., Venn, C. and Walkerdine, V. (1984) *Changing the Subject, Psychology, social regulation and subjectivity*. Methuen.

7   See Deem, R. (1978) *Women and Schooling* Routledge and Kegan Paul and Barrett, M. (1987) 'Gender and Class: Marxist feminist perspectives on education – section 3' in *Gender and the Politics of Schooling*.

8   See Kelly, A. (1987) 'The construction of masculine science' in *Gender and the Politics of Schooling*.

9   See Spender, D. (1982) 'Educational Institutions: Where Cooperation is Called Cheating' in Spender, D. and Sarah, E. (eds) *Learning to Lose* The Women's Press; Spender, D. (1987) 'Education: the patriarchal paradigm and the response to feminism' in *Gender and the Politics of Schooling*, Spender, D. (1982) 'The logic of dominance' in Spender, D. *Invisible Women: the schooling scandal*, Writers and Readers Cooperative.

10   For the relationship between judgements of 'real learning' and gender see Walden, R. and Walkerdine, V. (1985) *Girls and Mathematics*, Bedford Way Papers No 24, Institute of Education, University of London and Clarricoates, K. (1978, reprinted extract 1987), 'Dinosaurs in the classroom: the hidden curriculum in primary schools' in *Gender and the Politics of Schooling.*

11   For some analyses of the relationship between girls' education and the location of women in the family and the labour process see Deem, R. (ed) (1980) *Schooling for Women's Work*, Routledge and Kegan Paul.

12   The complexity of the cultural reproduction of gender positions and the crucial importance of sexuality in relation to schooling have been explored in Davies, L. (1984), *Pupil Power, Deviance and Gender in School*, Falmer Press; Lees, S. (1986) *Losing Out: sexuality and adolescent girls* Hutchinson; Wolpe, A. (1988) *Within School Walls: the role of discipline, sexuality and the curriculum*, Routledge.

13   The different positions of black females and white females are crucial here. The 'white view' of the construction of female sexuality and sexism, which may be responsible for its own stereotyping and subsuming of black famale experience, has justifiably been criticised by black females. See Carby, H. (1982) 'White woman listen! black feminism and the boundaries of sisterhood' in Centre for Contemporary Cultural Studies *The Empire Strikes Back*, Hutchinson.

14   I am indebted to my reading of the work of Valerie Walkerdine for the main substance of this section. See especially Walden, R. and Walkerdine, V. (1985) *Girls and Mathematics* Bedford Way Papers 24, Institute of Education, University of London; Walkerdine, V. (1985), 'On the regulation of speaking and silence' in Steedman, C., Urwin, C. and Walkerdine, V. (eds) *Language, Gender and Childhood*, Routledge and Kegan Paul; Walkerdine, V. (1981) 'Sex, power and pedagogy' Screen Education 38.

15   See Evans, G. (1988) 'Those Loud Black Girls' in Spender, D. and Sarah, E. (eds) *Learning to Lose* (revised edition 1988) and Riley, K. (1987) 'Black girls speak for themselves' in Weiner, G. (ed) *Just a Bunch of Girls*.

16   See (1989) *Discipline in Schools* Report of the Commitee of Enquiry chaired by Lord Elton HMSO.

17   My general approach to researching the classroom has been informed by reading Galton, M. (1987) 'An ORACLE chronicle: a decade of classroom research', in Delamont, S. (ed) *The Primary School Teacher*, Falmer Press and especially, Watkins, C. and Wagner, P. (1987) *School Discipline: a whole school approach*, Blackwell.

18   See Watkins, C. and Wagner, P. (1987) *School Discipline*, Blackwell.

19   For a discussion of a similar situation in an infant classroom see French, J. (1986) 'Gender and the classroom' in *New Society* 7 March 86.

20 See Schor, N. (1987) *Reading in Detail Aesthetics and the feminine* – introduction, Methuen.
21 See Kelly, A. (1987) 'The construction of masculine science' in *Gender and the Politics of Schooling*.
22 See Wilkinson L. C. and Marrett, C. B. (1985) *Gender Influences in Classroom Interaction*, Academic Press and Kelly, A. (1987) 'The construction of masculine science'.
23 See Watkins, C. and Wagner, P. (1987) *School Discipline: a whole school approach*, Blackwell.
24 See Clarricoates, K. (1987) 'Dinosaurs in the Classroom'.
25 See Mahoney, P. (1985) *School for the boys?: co-education re-assessed* Hutchinson.
26 Mahoney, P. *Schools for the boys?*
27 A considerable amount of research exists on male and female talk. Most useful for my purposes have been: Spender, D. (1982) 'Talking in Class' in *Learning to Lose* The Women's Press; Spender, D. (1980) 'The Dominant and the Muted' in Spender, D. *Man Made Language* Routledge and Kegan Paul; French, J. and French, P. (1984) 'Gender imbalances in the primary classroom: an interactional account', *Educational Research* 26:2; Coates, J. (1988) *Women, Men and Language*, Women's Press, also quoted in Claire, H. and Redpath, J. (1989) *Girls and Boys Interactions in the Primary Classroom*, Ealing Gender Equality Team; Bousted, M. (1989) 'Who talks? the position of girls in mixed sex classrooms', *English in Education*.
    Some of these have also informed my sections on teacher-pupil and pupil-pupil interaction.
28 The work of Barnes, Britton and Rosen is relevant here, although they do not deal with the gender implications of talk. See Barnes, D. Britton, J., Rosen, H. (1970) *Language, the Learner and the School* Penguin; Britton, J. (1970) *Language and Learning* Penguin.
29 See Wilkinson, L. C. and Marrett, C. B. (1985) *Gender Influences in Classroom Interaction* Academic Press.
30 See Spender, D. (1982) *Invisible women: the schooling scandal* Writers and Readers Co-op.; Stanworth, M. (1983) *Gender and Schooling: a study of sexual divisions in the classroom* Hutchinson.
31 See Clarricoates, K. (1987) 'Dinosaurs in the classroom' and Askew, S. and Ross, C. (1988) *Boys Don't Cry: boys and sexism in education*. Open University Press Gender and Education Series.
32 See Stanworth, M. (1983) *Gender and Schooling*.
33 See Wilkinson and Marrett (1985) and Askew and Ross (1988).
34 See Wilkinson and Marrett (1985) and Fuller, M. (1980) 'Black girls in a London comprehensive school' in Deem, R. (ed) *Schooling for Women's Work* Routledge and Kegan Paul.
35 See Wilkinson and Marrett (1985); Licht, B. and Dweck, C. (1987) 'Sex differences in achievement orientations' in *Gender and the Politics*

of Schooling; Davies, L. (1984) *Pupil Power, Deviance and Gender in School*; Stanworth, M. (1983) *Gender and Schooling*; Claire, H. and Redpath, J. (1989).

36 See Askew and Ross (1988).
37 See Stanworth, M. (1983).
38 See Bousted, M. (1989) 'Who talks?' and Claire, H. and Redpath, J. (1989).
39 See Davies, L. (1984).
40 See Clarricoates (1987) 'Dinosaurs in the classroom'; Stanworth, M. (1983); French, J. (1986); Askew and Ross (1988); Licht, B. and Dweck, C. (1987); Davies, L. (1984).
41 See Spender, D. (1982) *Invisible Women*.
42 See Bousted, M. (1989).
43 See Jones, C. (1987) 'Sexual tyranny: male violence in a mixed secondary school' in Weiner, G. (ed) *Just a Bunch of Girls* and Mahoney, P. (1985) *Schools for the boys?*
44 For the following observations on boys' competitiveness and their lack of co-operation skills see especially Askew and Ross (1988).
45 See Wilkinson and Marrett (1985).
46 See Wilkinson and Marrett (1985); Mahoney, P. (1985).
47 Bousted, M. (1989).
48 See Walden, R. and Walkerdine, V. (1985) *Girls and Mathematics* Bedford Way Papers No 24.
49 See Lees, S. (1986) *Losing Out* and Askew and Ross (1988).
50 Askew and Ross (1988).
51 See Claire, H. (1989) in Claire, H. and Redpath, J. *Girls' and Boys' Interactions in Primary Classrooms*.
52 See Lees, S. (1986) *Losing Out* and Davies, L. (1984).
53 The disadvantages to girls in working with boys is clearly demonstrated in Mahony, P. (1985).
54 See Mahony, P. (1985) for the arguments made against single-sex grouping and her counter arguments.

Bibliography

There is now quite an extensive literature on gender, schooling and classrooms. The following have been found most useful in researching for this chapter

Amos, V. and Parmar, P. (1987) 'Resistances and Responses: the experiences of black girls in Britain' in Arnot, M. and Weiner, G. (eds) *Gender and the Politics of Schooling*, Hutchinson/Open University.
Arnot, M. and Weiner, G. (1987) 'Teachers and Gender Politics' in *Gender and the Politics of Schooling* Hutchinson/Open University.

Askew, S. and Ross, C. (1988) *Boys Don't Cry: boys and sexism in education* Open University Press 'Gender and Education' Series.

Barnes, D., Britton, J., Rosen, H. (1970) *Language, the learner and the school* Penguin.

Brah, A. and Minhas, R. (1987) 'Structural Racism or Cultural Difference: Schooling for Asian Girls' in Weiner, G. (ed) *Just a Bunch of Girls* Open University Press 'Gender and Education' Series.

Britton, J. (1970) *Language and Learning* Penguin.

Bousted, M. (1989) 'Who talks? The position of girls in mixed sex classrooms' in *English in Education*.

Carby, H. (1982) 'White Woman Listen! Black Feminism and the Boundaries of Sisterhood' in Centre for Contemporary Cultural Studies *The Empire Strikes Back*, Hutchinson.

Claire, H. and Redpath, J. (1989) *Girls' and Boys' Interactions in Primary Classrooms*, Ealing Education Service, Gender Equality Team, Occasional Paper No 2.

Clarricoates, K. (1987) 'Dinosaurs in the Classroom: the hidden curriculum in primary schools' in Arnot, M. and Weiner, G. (eds) *Gender and the Politics of Schooling*, Hutchinson/Open University.

Coates, J. (1988) *Women, Men and language* Women's Press.

Committee of Enquiry chaired by Lord Elton (1989) *Discipline in Schools* HMSO.

Davies, L. (1984) *Pupil Power, Deviance and Gender in School* Falmer Press.

Deem, R. (ed) (1980) *Schooling for Women's Work* Routledge and Kegan Paul.

Evans, G. (1988) 'Those loud black girls!' in Spender, D. and Sarah, E. (eds), *Learning to Lose* Women's Press.

French, J. (1986) 'Gender and the classroom' in *New Society* 7 March 1986.

French, J. and French, P. (1984) 'Gender imbalances in the primary classroom, an interactional account' in *Educational Research* 26 No 2.

Fuller, M. (1980) 'Black girls in a London comprehensive school' in Deem, R. (ed) *Schooling for Women's Work* Routledge and Kegan Paul.

Galton, M. (1987) 'An ORACLE Chronicle – a decade of classroom research' in Delamont, S. (ed) *The Primary School Teacher* Falmer Press.

Henriques, J., Holloway, W., Urwin C., Venn, C. and Walkerdine, V. (1984) *Changing the Subject: psychology, social regulation and subjectivity* Methuen.

Inner London Education Authority (1981) *Achievement in schools: sex differences*, Report RS806/81.

Jones, C. (1987) 'Sexual Tyranny, male violence in a mixed secondary school' in Weiner, G. (ed) *Just a Bunch of Girls* Open University.

Kelly, A. (1987) 'The construction of masculine science' in Arnot, M. and Weiner, G. (eds) *Gender and the Politics of schooling* Hutchinson/Open University.

77

Lavigeur, J. (1982) 'Co-education and the tradition of separate needs' in Spender, D. and Sarah, E. (eds) *Learning to Lose* Women's Press.

Lees, S. (1986) *Losing Out: sexuality and adolescent girls* Hutchinson.

Licht, B. and Dweck, C. (1987) 'Sex differences in achievement orientations' in Arnot, M. and Weiner, G. (eds) *Gender and the Politics of Schooling* Hutchinson/Open University.

Mahony, P. (1985) *Schools for Boys?: co-education re-assessed*, Hutchinson.

Riley, K. (1987) 'Black girls speak for themselves' in Weiner, G. (ed) *Just a Bunch of Girls* Open University.

Schor, N. (1987) *Reading in detail: aesthetics and the feminine* Methuen.

Scott, M. (1982) 'Teach her a lesson: sexist curriculum in patriarchal education' in Spender, D. and Sarah, E. (eds) *Learning to Lose* Women's Press.

Spender, D. (1980) *Man Made Language* Routledge and Kegan Paul.

Spender, D. (1982) *Invisible Women: the schooling scandal* Writers and Readers Cooperative.

Spender, D. and Sarah, E. (1982) *Learning to Lose* Women's Press.

Stanworth, M. (1983) *Gender and Schooling: a study of sexual divisions in the classroom* Hutchinson.

Troyna, B. (ed) (1987) *Racial Inequality in Education* Tavistock Publications.

Walden, R. and Walkerdine, V. (1985) *Girls and Mathematics* Institute of Education. Bedford Way Papers No 24.

Walkerdine, V. (1981) 'Sex, power and pedagogy' *Screen Education* 38.

Walkerdine, V. (1985) 'On the regulation of speaking and silence' in Steedman, C., Urwin, C. and Walkerdine, V. (eds) *Language Gender and Childhood* Routledge and Kegan Paul.

Watkins, C. and Wagner, P. (1989) *School Discipline: a whole school approach* Blackwell.

Weiner, G. (1987) 'Equal Opportunities, Feminism and Girls' Education' in Weiner, G. (ed) *Just a Bunch of Girls*, Open University Press 'Gender and Education' Series.

Wilkinson, L. C. and Marrett, C. B. (1985) *Gender Influences in Classroom Interaction* Academic Press.

Williams, J. (1987) 'The construction of women and black students as educational problems: re-evaluating policy on gender and "race"' in Arnot, M. and Weiner, G. (eds) *Gender and the Politics of Schooling* Hutchinson/Open University.

Wolpe, A. (1988) *Within School Walls: the role of discipline, sexuality and the curriculum* Routledge.

SECTION TWO
PASTORAL ASPECTS OF
THE CURRICULUM

Introduction

Chris Watkins

Why is this section here?

In considering the impact a school has on the gender beliefs and behaviours of its pupils, the fact that pupils and teachers spend most of their time together in classrooms brings our attention to that setting. In classrooms, through both the planned and the unplanned interactions and experiences which take place, much of the school's impact is made. This section focuses on the planned learning offer in classrooms – ie, the curriculum. Some of the other processes of every classroom have been addressed in Jennifer Walden's chapter in Section 1. This examination will overlap to some extent with consideration in other sections; indeed, that must be the case, because pupils' learning is affected by them all.

The curriculum cannot be viewed in isolation from other features of a school. Pupils extract a range of social learnings from the major overlapping aspects of school. From the school organisation they learn about status, value, roles, hierarchy, and so on. From the school climate they learn about relationships, emotions, transactions between people. And from the school curriculum they learn the ideas and principles by which to understand their own and others' experience, and the skills to influence their own situations.

So, when we come to examine the gender aspects, it is clear that we must look at the curriculum in a whole-school, whole-person sense and must also recognise the overlap with school organisation and climate, (see Figure a).

It is important to identify the pastoral aspects of the curriculum in a whole-curriculum way. In other words, we must look at the *range* of social learnings which come from all parts of the planned learning offer, not merely some which are labelled in particular ways (tutorial programmes,

Figure a

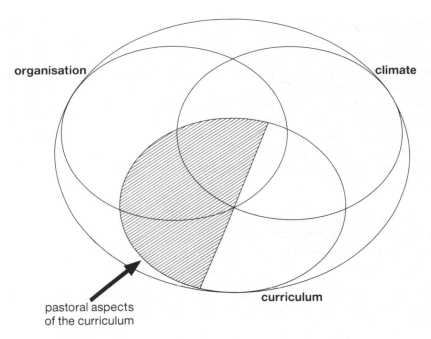

organisation

climate

pastoral aspects
of the curriculum

curriculum

timetabled PSE courses, or whatever). In this section we will not be using phrases such as the 'pastoral curriculum', in case they seem to imply that all the important learning can be squeezed into the marginal occasions which such phrases sometimes describe – at worst, 20 minutes tutorial time per week. Rather we will want to examine pastoral aspects of the whole-school curriculum. At times this will bring our attention to *all classrooms* and their contribution to personal-social learning – including gender processes (see Chapter 5).

In the last decade analysis has been undertaken of gender processes in most aspects of the curriculum, including most of the subjects. Yet it sometimes seems that little change has resulted from the increased awareness which this analysis has given us. If we think about gender attitudes in our society, or about the take-up of different subject routes by girls and boys, patterns remain broadly similar to those of a decade ago. We could attribute this to the fact that social change is a slow process, or that schools are not very powerful instruments in such social change, each of which is a reasonable view. But before we conclude that this is the whole picture, it may be profitable once again to look in detail at what schools can do, and in particular to look at curriculum design and delivery. Not much work of this sort has been undertaken in the pastoral aspects of the curriculum.

'But isn't this all off the agenda now?'

That is a question which colleagues have raised since the advent of the 'National' 'Curriculum', but a full reading of the facts shows that the answer is NO. The impetus to address the themes of this section could even be strengthened by developments associated with this legislation. The National Curriculum Council (NCC) has responsibility for advising on the *whole* curriculum (not just the attainment targets and so on); their remit includes taking account of the need for the school curriculum to promote *equality of opportunity for all pupils regardless of ethnic origin and gender*. Notwithstanding the fact that much of the early attention has been on particular subjects, the place of *cross-curricular dimensions* has been brought into focus. These are:

- personal-social education,
- equal opportunities, and
- multicultural education.

The report of the NCC's Interim Whole Curriculum Committee (unpublished, delivered to Secretary of State in April 1989) said:

> Personal and social education (PSE) is arguably the most important of the cross-curricular dimensions to which schools need to give attention. PSE can be seen as the promotion of the personal and social development of pupils through the school curriculum. It is concerned with fundamental educational aims and permeates the whole curriculum. It should be the responsibility of all teachers and a priority for school management.
>
> Personal and social education, in its broad sense, is part of every pupil's entitlement to a curriculum which promotes the purposes of education laid down by the Act. No component of the school curriculum is without its potential influence on personal and social development.

Thus the personal-social curriculum and its gender aspects are certainly still on the agenda, and it remains the responsibility of schools to analyse their practice and their curriculum in light of these dimensions.

But we should clearly recognise that there are hesitations and resistances to taking a direct approach on gender issues, whether in the context of personal-social education or not. In some schools it is still the case that explicit treatment of anti-sexist education is fought against, and in some schools first experiences in this area have led to disappointments. All the more reason to reassess what the school can do in a whole-school sense.

Returning to the national pronouncements on this area, the National Curriculum Council has not always been clear, and perhaps reflects hesitation or resistance. It has made one very confused statement on the relationship between personal-social education and gender issues. In their Circular number 6 (November 1989) *The National Curriculum and Whole Curriculum Planning* we read:

> Major cross-curricular dimensions which are not necessarily delivered through courses of personal and social education but which promote personal and social development include equal opportunities, and education for life in a multicultural society. (para 11)

There are a variety of interpretations which could be made of this:

If we forgot to stress the word 'necessarily', the statement could be seen as a suggestion for not addressing equal opportunities issues explicitly through PSE courses. As such it might attract a measure of support: anything which is addressed solely through PSE courses may become marginalised and therefore ineffective. Perhaps what is intended is a 'curriculum-wide' approach, with emphasis on the subjects. However, the circular continued:

> They require the development of positive attitudes in all staff and pupils towards cultural diversity, gender equality and people with disabilities.

This could be taken as a suggestion not to address equal opportunities issues through the curriculum at all, but reverting to the the nebulous notion of developing everybody's attitudes. As such it could be seen as a proposal for addressing cross-curricular dimensions without any reference to the curriculum! This would clearly be an untenable position, and is certainly not that adopted in this section.

As in all aspects of education, whether or not national bodies have got their thinking sorted out, practice in schools depends on teachers and the way they interpret and mediate their task.

What does this section offer?

First it offers the message that you, the reader, can do something to address gender issues through the pastoral aspects of the curriculum. This could be through a number of routes – in your classroom, in your tutorial occasion, in your team. Second, it offers some support in clarifying what the school can achieve through its curriculum. Getting this clear is a major step toward positive achievements in the area. Third, it stresses the need for a coordinated approach between all those contexts which have a curriculum impact. This is sorely needed across tutorial programmes, PSE courses, subject lessons, and so on. In this way we may ensure that our work is maximally effective, and we may avoid our attempts degenerating into an irrelevant competition over which of these contexts is 'best' for gender work.

What's in this section?

First a word on the terminology used. This book has consistently taken a whole-school use of the notion of pastoral care, and will continue to do so in its section on the curriculum. To signify this we use phrases such as 'the pastoral aspects of the curriculum' or 'personal-social aspects of the curriculum' to denote those parts of the whole-school curriculum where the personal and social aspects of pupils and their development is explicitly addressed in a planned and systematic way, *wherever* this occurs. We avoid use of the term 'pastoral curriculum' since we know that for some readers it implies a separation from the whole school curriculum, and for other readers it has become synonymous with tutorial programmes.

In the first chapter issues are raised concerning appropriate goals for explicit gender work, and a view of appropriate goals is put forward. The content and location of pastoral aspects of the curriculum are addressed, followed by ideas on constructing appropriately-structured activities for direct classroom work. Gill Venn gives an account of work in a particular programme, which led her to question the espoused aims. She demonstrates that activity-based work implies an active role for the teacher in structuring the learning occasion, and she includes a focus on pupils' evaluations of their experience in some sorts of groupwork.

Sue Askew and Carol Ross argue against an isolated 'pastoral curriculum' and propose a whole-school view which recognises the special role and function of the tutor. They outline the relationship between personal-social education goals and issues of inequality, and indicate the problems with using a separate course of PSE to address equal opportunities issues. Again this raises issues about how realistic goals are, the need to address real situations in direct work, the need to address transfer of learning in a concrete and practical way, and the need to examine situations in and around the school and the messages in the institution itself. In their whole-school view the tutor has a key role in overseeing pupils' progress, and in mediating between pupils and aspects of the school.

5

What can the pastoral aspects of the curriculum contribute?

Chris Watkins

This chapter has two main aims:

1 To examine and discuss what are feasible goals for us to adopt (and try to achieve) when we give an explicit treatment to gender themes in the pastoral aspects of the curriculum.
2 To identify some of the principles we could profitably employ when devising and doing such work with pupils.

The chapter starts by looking at *goals* for the pastoral or personal-social aspect of the curriculum, and examines six versions of goals as they are talked about by teachers and others. These are discussed and evaluated, and an effective approach to goals is suggested. Then the parallels for work on gender issues are drawn, and suggestions made as to what would be appropriate and feasible goals in this area.

The second section develops pointers for practice in classrooms, by looking at the ways in which we attempt to achieve the goals through classroom work and classroom activities. The final section makes some suggestions for devising materials in this area, and shows how particular examples were designed.

In writing this chapter I am hoping to offer some possible clarifications to any colleague who is interested in working on gender themes. My motivation for this springs from numerous experiences where teachers who have a genuine commitment to improving gender equity have had disappointing experiences when they have tried out direct work in the classroom. I have often felt that this disappointment could have been avoided had there been more in-depth discussion of goals and more detailed attention given to learning experiences.

Goals and the pastoral aspects of the curriculum

This section attempts some clarifications which I believe are greatly needed. As the introduction [pp 80–84] to this part of the book has pointed out, widely differing notions of curriculum exist in our schools today, especially in the personal-social aspects. This is of concern, because the diversity of views is not one which reflects clearly thought-out different rationales: it is more often the product of confusions and of 'knock-on effects' resulting from decisions taken elsewhere in school. This state of affairs is compounded rather than clarified by the range of different approaches schools are adopting toward personal-social education (in its whole-school sense) in the context of the National Curriculum. The pastoral aspects of the curriculum are often under-organised, under-resourced, and under-managed.

There is a similarly diverse picture in the *goals* which are supposedly being achieved through this aspect of school. Discussions about the personal-social and gender are often unprofitable because there is an un-examined range of views about what it is right to achieve, and what it is possible to achieve.

In attempting to clarify some points about goals, I do not intend to imply that this will be the major way to improve practice – too much time talking about goals could lead us into interminable discussions about 'the aims of education', and we could fall into the trap of portraying teachers and schools as highly planned. In reality, our practice is affected by many influences other than our plans alone. Also, there will always be divergence amongst teachers with respect to goals – perhaps more so in personal-social areas – because our goals as teachers reflect in part our personal perspectives, our own social experiences, our world-views, and so on. But there *is* value to be gained from starting off with a degree of analysis in this area: it promotes a discussion of important issues and can provide a context for various views to be examined. We might find we have adopted goals which, with more reflection, we would not have espoused. It is this refining of our rationale for our intervention in personal-social areas which the discussion stimulates. It does not bring a 100% consensus. Our overall aim is that of goal clarification, not a complete consensus. And in the process of reflecting on curriculum aims each of us may unearth some of our unstated aims.

The espoused aims in the pastoral aspects of curriculum are described and talked about in a variety of ways. I characterise a number below, aware that such characterisation may contain a hint of exaggeration, but hoping that readers may be able to identify aspects of each in daily examples in their working context.

Omnipotent goals

Here we find people talking about their goals in a way which overstates their possible impact as teachers, together perhaps with too little questioning of their right to be intervening in this area. Extreme examples include 'to correct self image' (Davies). This is a distortion because schools do not have a simple or direct impact on their students' self-images; rather they have a slow, cumulative effect on particular aspects of pupils' views of themselves (for example their view of their own abilities in certain school subjects). This comes about through a combination of factors rather than through the direct attempts of teachers to influence them. Other examples are contained in suggestions that this part of the curriculum has some meaningful contribution to 'changing society'. In 45 minutes a week?!

Rather than fall into the trap of overestimating our direct influence, any serious approach to personal-social education in a plural society demands that teachers try to question their views and their judgments of pupils rather than attempt to impose those views in some indirect way through the curriculum.

Romantic goals

The main feature here is an over-emphasis on the positive, the 'nice' things in life, with the assumption (generally unstated) that a focus of this sort will somehow provide a positive learning experience. It is possible to identify underlying messages which seem to say 'Let's all be friendly and cooperative' – this could be merely romantic, as could 'Let's look at how we get on in families, and how we can all get on better'. The trap of course is that this attitude can become like that of 'Pollyanna' with teachers making excessive efforts to find something positive in even the worst situations. The result may be to avoid examination of conflicts, difficulties and negative experiences which occur in pupils' lives, and to inadvertently imply that there are no ways of dealing with these things. Sometimes this approach is based on a misunderstanding of such ideas as 'enhancing self-esteem', and a mistaken belief that teachers can help their students feel positive about themselves by addressing only the positive features of their experience. In the worst cases this can generate a very cosy and sometimes cloying feeling.

Conversion goals

Goals of this sort usually rest on an idea that pupils are approaching or understanding some issue in an incorrect way, and that if we can give them some convincing demonstration (of the error of their ways) they will 'see the light' and accordingly adjust their approach. We can see examples of this when the learning occasions aim 'to show...' or 'to demonstrate...' or 'to get the pupils to see...' something which the teachers have decided is important. This leaves out two very important considerations. First, the underlying message is that the pupils are wrong; pupils will quickly perceive this message and react accordingly, probably with disengagement. Second, it does not follow that if a pupil (or anyone else for that matter) sees that an approach is ineffective they will be able to then develop an effective approach – much more detailed and practical work is needed in order to develop new strategies.

Amorphous goals

These can be identified by their generality and lack of analysis. For example a goal such as 'to *discuss*...[a particular theme or issue]' can lead to an experience where pupils engage in a generalised conversation, and do not necessarily find the structure to analyse, apply or develop new approaches. Pupils end up with a situation which lacks rigour or depth. Moreover, amorphous approaches may just as likely provide an arena where pupils' existing strategies are reinforced rather than reviewed, rehearsed and supported rather than examined and analysed. In groups, unstructured discussion can lead to destructive outcomes such as scapegoating and other forms of attack. Discussion by itself does not necessarily provide a learning experience: structured discussion, application and transfer of learning is required.

Insular goals

Sometimes the purposes can focus on the individual pupil or the small (tutorial) group to an excessive degree, thereby excluding a proper consideration of influences and processes outside. For example, approaches which aim to help adolescents examine aspects of their behaviour through much use of 'self-assessments' of a particular sort may appear to explain pupil behaviour by recourse to 'the self' of the pupil. If over-done this omits consideration of the context, and inadvertently implies that the cause is located within the individual pupil. This could become individualistic, and would omit a proper examination of all the social and societal processes which influence the development of self in the fullest sense. Another example of insular goals can be found in those approaches to the tutor group which overestimate the importance of that particular grouping (which pupils did not choose, and which is likely to have its fair share of sub-groups). It is possible to forget that pupils spend their time in many other groupings. The pitfall here is that of becoming too introspective, focusing too much on the individual or the group, without giving enough consideration to the context of school, family, community and so on. Investigation of those contexts is vital if learning is to transfer: people are not enabled to make the changes they desire without focusing on the context where the changes are to take place.

Antidote goals

Here the goals are set by reference to supposed deficiencies elsewhere – in the pupils' school or other experience. For example, some goals for narrower approaches to 'study skills' are justified on the basis that processes of learning are not examined in the subject lessons. And sometimes a focus on personal-social education in separate timetabled occasions is justified because it is said not to form a part of experience elsewhere on the timetable. More wide-ranging examples include those where the school sets itself up in an unexamined way to remedy supposed deficits in the pupils' home experience: 'pupils from these backgrounds/this community need this sort of education' you can hear said – a view which might be founded on inaccurate stereotypes which systematically underestimate the strengths of the home. Whichever example of antidote thinking it is, goals of this sort will fall into the trap of overestimating their own possibilities and not give sufficient importance to learning about the real processes elsewhere.

The advantage to be gained from identifying pitfalls is that one can subsequently recognise them as they are about to arise. It is then possible to avoid them. If we take the six types of goals listed above, and identify what sort of goals will *not* fall into those traps, we will have identified a powerful set of goals for this aspect of the curriculum.
Characteristics would be:

* recognising and examining the real influences in pupils' lives, rather than simple or direct influence attempts;
* addressing the difficult processes and feelings as well as the positives;
* helping pupils develop and extend, from their motivations – not converting them from wrong thinking;
* a clear focus on action and particular strategies to develop, not just talk;
* investigating issues in the context of school, home etc, not focusing only on self or the small group;
* engaging a number of contexts and using the strengths they contribute, rather than trying to make up for deficits elsewhere.

If we develop the personal-social aspects of our curriculum with goals which are characterised by the above list, I believe that it could honestly deserve the title of an *empowering* curriculum. As such it would be helping pupils develop their understandings and strategies in a realistic and contextualised way. And it would refute some of those ill-informed accusations which are sometimes targeted on personal-social education, for example, that it is some sort of social engineering. These are over-blown critiques which over-estimate the power of the curriculum anyway. Certainly the sort of curriculum being envisaged here does not aim to encourage conformist allegiance to anything! Nor (on the other hand) does it believe that some sort of revolutionary change can come about through educational processes. Similarly, talk of social engineering assumes that teachers could somehow decide how to influence their pupils in some particular social direction. This is unrealistic. It does not take seriously the fact that teachers have little

Figure 5.1

	Focusing on society	Focusing on individuals
Concerned to initiate change	*Social change* To help students see the need for political and social change and to develop the relevant action skills	*Individual change* To maximise the life-chances of the individual within society
Not concerned to initiate change	*Social control/ socialisation* To initiate students into societal norms related to work, family and citizenship	*Non-directive, pro-autonomy* To encourage informed autonomous choice of social lifestyle

direct general influence on their pupils in the personal-social domain. It contains echoes of past, unrealistic talk of teachers as 'indoctrinators'.

At this point it may be useful to remind ourselves that in the search for a realistic statement of goals it is possible to get the balance wrong in a variety of ways (as the examples above are intended to point out). The work of Rosemary Lee[1] gives a particularly useful analysis which is relevant both to the present day education system, and to the gender issues we are about to address.

Lee suggested four possible aims of social education programmes: (see Figure 5.1) This diagram of possible aims helps in two ways: first we can identify various goals and realise that a sole focus on any one type would be ineffective; second we can look at any particular school programme and assess the balance of its contribution in these four types.

Applying these ideas to a curriculum on gender

In developing a set of appropriate goals to inform our curriculum work on gender themes and issues, it is possible to identify particular examples of the six pitfalls listed in general terms in the previous section. For example

- Omnipotent goals: to *correct* gender identity?
- Romantic goals: to be *happy* about gender differences?

- Conversion goals: to *demonstrate* gender inequalities?
- Amorphous goals: to *discuss* gender issues?
- Insular goals: to *reflect on* our own gender?
- Antidote goals: to *make up for* the fact that no-one else discusses gender?!

Before we jump to reject these entirely, let us recognise that there may be an element of each which attracts us, and which may attract our colleagues. On occasion it's very understandable that we wish we had some greater influence, but that is hardly the role of the curriculum for adolescents. We could easily fall into replicating the way in which some adults attempt to exercise a controlling power over some young people, and that would negate the very learning we aim to encourage.

Instead, let us again take the characteristics which these pitfalls help us identify, and develop more appropriate goals of the following style:

1 To help pupils assess gender influences on them and on others they know
2 To examine gender discrimination and the feelings which arise from it
3 To examine the gains to be made from greater gender equity, eg in relationships
4 To look closely at particular issues and to develop appropriate action on gender issues
5 To investigate gender issues in the contexts of school and community
6 To learn about gender in a range of school settings, utilising the strengths which have been identified in each

A curriculum with these goals can be very empowering to young people, with an appropriate balance being struck between the focus on individual and the focus on society, and between initiating change and not initiating change. Our programmes should also strike a balance between three important aspects of:

Feeling
Thinking
Doing

These three inter-relate to a marked degree, and an over-emphasis on one to the detriment of the others will not be effective.

What can the pastoral aspects of the curriculum deliver?

Given the broad goals which have been developed above, we can now move to specify some of the *content* which our curriculum may address. In a later section we shall look at the processes of learning, but it is important to get a sense of the content too – otherwise we may fall into a particular difficulty for this work, that of appearing to say that 'it's all process'. Certainly the content is not going to be a body of facts (nor, even, facts about the body), but there are understandings, skills, and awareness which we can specify.

Taking each of the above goal statements in turn, it is clear that some lead directly to teaching aims and some also lead to aims about the way we organise our teaching in this area.

1 *To help pupils assess gender influences on them and on others they know.* This would give rise to learning about who are the real influences. The influence of parents, peers, teachers, and other elements in society can be addressed through small case studies of a young person in relation to each of these. Further work could be stimulated by examining data which shows the gender patterns in various choices and decisions, and raising the question of how to explain these patterns and influences.

2 *To examine gender discrimination and the feelings which arise from it.* Some teachers may shy away from the negative feelings which our pupils clearly experience as a result of various discriminations made against them. Rather than defensively 'sweeping them under the carpet' we need to engage in slow, patient work so that these feelings can be recognised and addressed. Again, carefully controlled case studies may be a method for serious examination of such issues. It is clear that adolescents are able to develop an extended sensitivity to the dynamics which devalue others: teaching which supports this development will need to do it with detail, and must not be made trivial by accepting defensive generalisations ('oh, that doesn't matter – boys are like that' and so on). When addressing gender stereotypes which are imposed by influential others, teachers will need to be supportive to young people who are challenging such influences: this may feel uncomfortable at first.

3 *To examine the gains to be made from greater gender equity eg in relationships.* Some work on gender can break down at this point. Unless we have a vision of how increased gender equity can lead to gains for both men and women, we will not convey any sense of gain to the young people who might profit from questioning a traditional view of gender differences. Greater emotional health, a wider range of choice, relationships which are not dominated by stereotype and power – these are some of the gains for both men and women which need to be examined. Adolescents in particular are likely to view as a gain the chance to examine the choices which feel right for them, without feeling pressured by others' expectations.

4 *To look closely at particular issues and to develop appropriate action on gender issues.* Here we can start to anticipate some of the gender themes and issues in which pupils may wish to feel more skilled and competent,

and in which action may be taken (on some occasions by them and on other occasions by their teachers). These themes are likely to be a particular set of the themes which we find in adolescent personal-social development. Here they are ordered under a set of headings which applies more generally to personal-social education:

- *bodily self*: major issues of body image and how these are affected by gender stereotype; coping with talk about body image
- *sexual self*: relation between gender and sexuality; stereotypes about what are appropriate gender roles in sexual relations
- *social self*: social relations between the sexes; the implications of being 'masculine' or 'feminine' in social relations; assertiveness
- *vocational self*: expectations of what roles and areas are gender appropriate, moving into non-traditional work and non-work roles
- *moral/political self*: examining one's own judgments and the degree to which they are affected by stereotypes such as gender; making moral judgments about issues which relate to gender; examining how to change what has been judged as wrong
- *self as a learner*: expectations and aspirations in learning: patterns of difference in learning
- *self in the organisation*; different expectations which the school has for males/females; different patterns of behaviour by males/females in classrooms, playgrounds, staff etc.

5 *To investigate gender issues in the contexts of school and community.* This issue has been implied in the list above, in other words, that the gender issues which are evident in the school context are worthy of investigation as part of the educative process. It is an obvious step to take the same process beyond the walls of the school.

6 *To learn about gender in a range of school settings, utilising the strengths which have been identified in each.* This issue will be further addressed in the following section.

Where are the various pastoral contributions?

The strategy in this section of the book has been to consider pastoral aspects of the curriculum in a whole-school way, in order to take account of the various locations where a contribution is made to pupils' learning about themselves and about personal-social behaviour and issues. Now that appropriate goals for that curriculum and its gender aspects have been discussed, it might be fruitful to address some further points regarding this learning offer. In particular, we need to examine issues about how such a learning offer may be distributed and coordinated.

Typically we might think of these 'locations':

- tutorial periods, tutorial time on the timetable
- specialist lessons eg Careers, Health, PSE (if done by a specialist team)
- subect lessons (both particular ones specified for their likely contribution, and all lessons for their wider contribution)
- work experience, residential experience
- school climate (including public status events such as assemblies) and the opportunity structure the school provides for pupils

In many schools you can find teachers arguing over which of these is the 'best' location. That is a regrettable waste of their energy, since it misses some fundamental points. Themes and issues which have implications for gender in our society arise in very many situations, and they will arise in many school situations. Therefore we need a two-pronged approach in school: on one hand to develop everyone's awareness of these issues in a range of everyday school contexts [these themes are addressed in other sections of this volume], and on the other to plan the learning offer for pupils. But we should be clear that the latter approach will also examine the situations pupils experience in the school: this will include their experiences in all classrooms. It follows that to have the learning offer on such a broad theme addressed in one location is unlikely to be very effective [as argued by Sue Askew and Carol Ross in a following chapter]. In particular it will not be effective to locate all this work in a marginalised and under-resourced tutorial programme (which is what many of them are). Rather we need to consider what themes may best be addressed, in what locations, by what teams; in this discussion we need to clarify what the special contribution of the tutorial programme might be. Then we may utilise a number of locations in a more effective and coordinated way.

Tutorial programmes offer advantages of the following sorts:

1   The tutor has a link with parents through a range of communication and meetings (including the school's parents' evenings if they are effectively organised). Thus the tutor may have an understanding of the parents' views about the pupil, including views which may be discussed as a gender theme, eg views about future careers, options, learning and many more.

2   The tutor has a cross-subject view of each pupil. This puts the tutor in a unique and important position when it comes to talking about different experiences of learning, the pupil's preferred styles of learning, and being a proactive learner.

94

3 The tutor has a cumulative relationship with the pupil, possibly developing over five years. This means that the tutor has an important perspective on the pupil's development and this should be engaged in discussions about development.
4 The tutor's interactions with the pupil are in a context which is not dominated by syllabus demands. Thus teachers may feel more able to facilitate reflective discussions at the pupils' pace (as long as their meetings are not over-programmed by worksheets from someone else!).
5 The tutor is given a guidance/overview function towards the group. This is increasingly referred to by HMI[2] and National Curriculum Council[3]. The main areas of guidance are reviewing and supporting school progress, planning future pathways, and so on.

Planning the learning offer

We now turn to some practical considerations which may well be appropriate for all teacher teams when considering and planning their contribution to the overall learning offer in the personal-social domain. First some points about the general orientation which is useful when approaching such planning.

Planning for competence and avoiding the pitfalls

One of the key issues in designing a curriculum which is really empowering is being clear about the competences which the learning aims to develop. If we focus on competences and skills we are likely to avoid the pitfalls which have been outlined in the first section of this chapter – moralising, converting, and so on.

There are some useful guiding principles when devising a string of learning experiences in this way:

1 Ask yourself *What competences and skills would these young people wish to extend?* in the general area under consideration. Taking the question seriously will reduce the risk of attempts at imposition, and will increase our chances of engaging with the real motivations of our pupils. Sometimes teachers give a cynical laugh when asked to raise this question on themes of gender, but the laugh usually indicates their lack of ease in another area – that of sexuality.

It is indeed possible to ask adolescents directly which of a range of areas they would prioritise for attention. This can be done through a discussion group if the relationships have been well developed. On some occasions this task can be stimulated and helped by a structured task: a format such as that in Figure 5.2 could be effectively adapted for particular groups and themes.

2   Ask yourself *What significant other people are these competences to be directed towards?* This will remind us to keep a focus on interactions with people who really are significant in the young people's worlds, probably parents and peers. Then we may avoid trivialising the competences (as happens, for example, when assertiveness training spends most of its time focusing on interactions with waiters and shop assistants, rather than addressing the more significant interactions with closer people). And we may also avoid giving too great a role to people who are not significant, particularly teachers.

3   The third guiding question is *In what situations does the need for this competence arise?* This principle helps us arrive at a suitably detailed focus. When we know what competences adolescents would wish to extend, towards which significant people, in what situations we have a good starting point for addressing skills in a suitably detailed manner and are then more likely to be practical and helpful.

With this background we can move on to more detailed planning. Some of the issues which need to be addressed are grouped here into two main areas: first the handling of classrooms and of classroom groups; second the construction and use of materials which may stimulate learning in such groups.

Classroom work in groups

Using small group activities
If teachers want to raise themes and encourage pupils to examine their strategies in a number of areas, this is most unlikely to be achieved in a whole-class setting of up to 30 pupils. Rather, the classroom setting will need to be sensitively organised to generate small group work and structured activities which provide the arena for pupils to examine issues and strategies. We do not use activity-based groupwork because it's a new fashion (it's not!); we use it because of what we know about learning, and the goals we have clarified for this work. Specifically

1   *To maximise learners' involvement and engagement in the learning process* We want learners to be engaged on as many dimensions as possible, in order that their learning is maximised, and their chance of remembering is also increased; we do not want them to be passive receivers.

2   *To give room for learners to explore their views, their relevances, and applications to their situations which they judge appropriate* We do not set ourselves up as simple influences on pupils: rather, we aim to arrange situations in which they can choose to examine their present views and

Figure 5.2

A survey of some of your skills

How good are you at each of the things in this list?
Circle the number on the right that shows how good you
think you are at each one.

1 means something I am NEVER good at
2 means something I am SELDOM good at
3 means something I am SOMETIMES good at
4 means something I am USUALLY good at
5 means something I am ALWAYS good at

a.	Starting a conversation	1 2 3 4 5
b.	Giving people compliments	1 2 3 4 5
c.	Apologising if I've done something wrong	1 2 3 4 5
d.	Showing people I'm annoyed with them	1 2 3 4 5
e.	Handling pressure from others	1 2 3 4 5
f.	Showing people I like them	1 2 3 4 5
g.	Talking to people of the other sex	1 2 3 4 5
h.	Deciding on the job I want	1 2 3 4 5

Now add four items of your own which are important to
you, and circle the number that shows how good you
think you are at them:

i.	1 2 3 4 5
j.	1 2 3 4 5
k.	1 2 3 4 5
l.	1 2 3 4 5

Last, write down here the letters of the three items that
you would most like to be more effective at:

(a)
(b)
(c)

[adapted from Priestley and McGuire, 1981[4]]

approaches, reflect on them and the influences which exist on them, and decide whether they wish to apply any new-found ideas or strategies to their own situation. It is they, not us, who have the responsibility for action, and it is they who will take new ideas into their own lives. This applied sort of education needs activity-based exploration and activity-based preparation, and this will be best achieved in small pupil groupings.

3 *To emphasise that there is no 'one right answer' but numerous personally valid solutions* In all aspects of the personal-social, teachers are rightly doubtful about being set up as 'experts' in whatever knowledge is implied. None of us are expert in running our own lives and with the uniqueness of our lives there are no simple answers to be offered. Thus small-group methods where the pupils are supported in examining a range of approaches are appropriate, with the tutor facilitating the groups rather than supplying 'answers'.

4 *To encourage a process of experimentation and change* Experimentation and change is a hallmark of healthy adolescence; it is the process of trying out a strategy, receiving feedback from others, and developing new approaches. Activity-based methods mirror and support this process. As such they need to make explicit reference to new strategies and behaviours to try out, and set targets for experimenting with a change.

5 *To examine social processes through the simulation of, and reflection on those processes* Developing one's view of oneself and the strategies one feels comfortable with is centrally a social process: it would be absurd to try to address these issues by merely talking about them. Rather we use small group activities where pupils have to involve themselves in examples of social situations and then reflect upon what has happened to them. In this way their whole experience is engaged.

Adopting a person-centred approach

Much of the earlier discussion on appropriate goals clarified that there is little mileage in approaches which are based on direct influence attempts by the teacher – the 'telling' or 'selling' approaches to personal-social development. The above points on activity-based groupwork have suggested a more effective, manageable and structured approach to person-centred work in a classroom setting.

Engaging the interpersonal influences

If we take seriously the teacher's role of facilitating social learning, we will find ourselves considering with pupils the range of influences on their views about issues involving gender. This is necessary for a realistic approach. But we need to approach the task in a suitably sophisticated way. The views of parents and peers are not simply adopted by young people; they are examined, reacted to, modified and so on. Therefore we will find the teacher asking young people to talk about their parents' and peers' views, how they respond to them, and the similarities and differences which arise.

Constructing materials

One aspect of such classroom-based work is the stimulus materials that may be used. Published examples are not in plentiful supply,[5] and it may be that teachers decide to devise their own materials. What follows in this section are some possible ingredients from a particular set of materials[6] which have received positive evaluations in use. The pupil materials (minus their excellent cartoons and separated from the teacher and other materials) are reproduced at the end of this chapter as Pupil Material examples 1 to 5).

1 Devise activities which engage the influential people in the pupil's lifespace. Major characters might be those shown in the simplified lifespace diagram below (Figure 5.3); we could write activities which examine issues in any of these relationships (or combinations of them).
2 Devise activities which address a realistic situation: one which feels 'live' to pupils and which contains an issue they would wish to handle effectively. Situations which contain an important tension or which are possibly embarrassing are worth considering here, since they encapsulate an issue and the people with whom that issue is salient.
3 Keep a focus on action, giving explicit attention to the strategies which pupils might adopt. Consideration of these can be triggered by discussion of 'What shall I do?' and 'What shall I say?', and can be developed by examining alternative answers. When writing activities which offer a

Figure 5.3

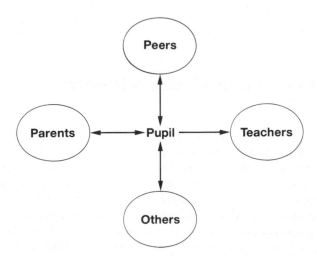

list of possible responses to start off the process, it is always important to include consideration of 'socially non-desirable alternatives' (in other words the actions which teachers might disapprove of) for two reasons. First, the credibility of the exercise – it is all too easy to destroy this and elicit from pupils the responses which they think teachers want (see examples in Gill Venn's chapter). Second, if there are in your view non-desirable alternatives, it is important that young people get time to examine these themselves and develop their own view (they'll be doing this anyway when you're not there!). Examples 1 and 2 use lists of alternatives for pupils to address: other examples use more open questions.

4 Develop a structured discussion to follow up the examination of the situation. This can be achieved by asking pupils to look for similarities and differences between their approaches, to address the reasons they give for what happens, to examine costs and consequences of their choices, and so on.

5 Consider the transfer of learning, and the setting up of experiments in an explicit way with pupils. This can be stimulated through questions such as 'What other situations do you know that are like this one we've been looking at?', 'What strategies have you learned today which might apply in that situation?', 'Is there an experiment we can try before next time?', 'What observations shall we do before next time?'

Finally some goal setting may be relevant, asking pupils to say to each other what they intend to do before the next session on the issues which have been raised in this one.

With the above ingredients, activity-based learning can be effective. We may come to ask the important question: 'Will the pupils feel more competent at something by the end of these activities?' not, 'Did we change the world?' [If you ask the former you may surprise yourself by getting a positive answer to the latter – even though it's not all at once!]

Issues in teams developing this work

Having set the scene for development, it is worthwhile recognising that such development is likely to be going on amongst groups or teams of teachers. Indeed it is necessary for teachers to work on gender themes together, so that ideas are tested and developed further. But things are not always simple or smooth. This final section aims to anticipate some of the issues and dynamics which may surface in such teams, so that colleagues may recognise them as pitfalls and then aviod them. This is in the spirit of the whole of this chapter, which is to address likely difficulties and thereby reduce the chance that our work may be made impotent by such difficulties when they arise.

1   Guilt. In areas such as sexism and racism there is an easily-triggered dynamic which says 'You (men, or whites, or white men) are the ones who are causing this distress – you should feel sorry for what you've done'. If this happens it can reduce the chances of those same men/whites taking positive action to improve matters – they can be paralysed by the overstated and individualistic sense of responsibility which makes up guilt. Instead, we have to recognise the historical and social processes which have landed us where we are, and recognise that change will take time.

2   Blame is in a way another side of the guilt coin. It can be destructive in considering gender matters because it is again based on an over-simplified attribution of cause. 'I blame the boys' may provide a neat pseudo-explanation, but may serve to bury questions such as 'What processes on the girls' parts may serve to maintain these patterns?'. To examine this sort of question without seeing it as yet another blaming issue may develop important perspectives and possibilities for change. 'I blame them' may generate safe feeling in the speaker, but may also reduce their responsibility in changing matters.

3   Harsh judgment is probably involved in each of the above, and it is often an ingredient when a group becomes polarised. There are well-worn dimensions for polarisation when gender is discussed: there are also long-standing feelings which may be driving harsh judgments. As is the case for pupils, teams must give themselves time and the appropriate climate in which to understand each others' views and arrive at a working consensus.

4   Forgetting the point is a process which in a way this whole chapter has been aiming to combat. In gender aspects of the curriculum the discussion in teams can lead to important issues which could take teachers into many fundamental areas. But the point is to devise curriculum for the pupils, and a balance must be kept between the proper discussion of team members' perspectives and planning the team's activity with the pupils. It is often worth remembering that the important discussion which teachers may find themselves moving into is the very discussion they were hoping to develop with the pupils. This helps us remember the point that our overall goal is to provide occasions when pupils may develop new practical competences.

In closing this chapter I can only say that I wish you, the reader, success in whatever developments you aim to set off. I hope the chapter has helped by providing some structured points to address. I hope I haven't used the word 'pitfall' too much, thereby unintentionally giving the message that this is an extremely treacherous area to enter! Rather, I hope to have conveyed the message that productive and active work is indeed possible, that its contribution to developing improved social equity is worthwhile, and that while it does not change the world overnight it is an essential aspect of the school's work.

Examples of Pupil Material

The following pages give some examples of material on gender/equal opportunities themes which are designed for use with pupils, the design of which has been referred to in this chapter.

References

1   Lee, R. (1980) *Approaches to Social Education* Further Education Unit.
2   HMI (1989) *Personal and Social Education 5 to 16*, Curriculum Matters series, DES.
3   National Curriculum Council (1989) *Interim report of whole curriculum committee*.
4   McGuire, J. and Priestley, P. (1981) *Life After School: a social skills curriculum* Pergamon.
5   See the resources listing in this volume.
6   'Equal Opportunities: What's in it for boys?', a pack of materials devised by Anne Carter, Frances Magee, Les Mapp, Kate Myers, Ross Rospigliosi and Chris Watkins originally published by ILEA/Schools Council reprinted 1988 by Whyld Publishing.

Example 1

Why bother with this?
– to think about how some boys end up acting tough when they don't really want to
– to find some other ways of acting

Tony is in the first year and is having a bit of difficulty with a boy from the third year. This boy, Alan, keeps on bothering Tony by nicking sweets, and now he's saying he wants 10 pence and he'll clobber Tony if he doesn't hand it over tomorrow.

Tony doesn't know what to do.

His Dad has always taught him to fight back with people like this: maybe he'll risk getting a bloody nose (Alan's bigger).

His teachers have told Tony that they must be told about things like this: maybe he'll risk being seen as a creep.

His friends in the first year don't seem to have so much difficulty with blokes like Alan: maybe he'll have to do something like they do – but what?

Inside, Tony doesn't feel like being 'tough'.

- What would happen if you were to:
  a) do nothing
  b) act upset
  c) talk to your form tutor
  d) find some mates to help get Alan
  e) be prepared to fight back
  f) have a go at Alan first
  g) not come to school the next day
  h) give him 5p and say that's all he'll get
  i) think why Alan's picking on you and find a way to change it

- Discuss your answers in groups of six. What would happen next?

Example 2

What's the point of this?
– to look at how talk between groups of boys can sometimes create
  difficulties
– and to find ways round those difficulties

The situation:

> Wayne is nattering with his mates at breaktime. Brian and
> Winston have started talking about the two girls they met
> yesterday evening. Brian reckons that the girl he was with
> 'might be a goer', and Winston says that the girl he was with
> 'wouldn't let me explore her'.
>
> Wayne feels uncomfortable because he doesn't talk about the
> girls he meets in that way, and he knows he would feel even
> worse if his friend Jane was being talked about like that. He
> wants to find a way of stating his point of view, but is a bit
> afraid that he'll be seen as someone who's not interested in
> girls.

● Discuss in groups of four: What could Wayne say?

● What do you think would happen if Wayne said:
  a) that he didn't think the girls would like their com-
      ments
  b) that he thought Brian and Winston were showing off
  c) nothing
  d) that he knew other things about the two girls
  e) that Brian and Winston should shut up

● How can Wayne best handle the impression that his
  mates might have?

Example 3

What's the point of this?
– to consider how some girls may have expectations of how boys behave

The situation:

> Jerry is talking with Sandra about what they're going to do next Saturday evening. They both have Saturday jobs – Sandra works in an ironmongers' shop and Jerry in a hairdressers – so have agreed that going to the pictures might be the best thing...
>
> Sandra: 'I don't mind which film I see, Jerry. I'll be happy to go to the one you want to see'
> Jerry: 'Well, I didn't have a particular one in mind – I see the latest Indiana Jones is on: do you like those?'
> Sandra: 'Yes if you do. I don't mind'
> Jerry: 'Well I suppose I've seen the others. There's a new horror movie at the Odeon – what about that?'
> Sandra: 'Yes, alright: whatever you decide. After all, it's you that's taking me out...'

1 In pairs, with one person as Jerry, and the other as Sandra, carry on the conversation above, for two minutes.
   ● What happens, and why?
   ● Discuss: why Sandra is behaving like this
              how it makes Jerry feel

2 Now change roles – the person who was Jerry is now Sandra, and vice versa. Carry on the above conversation again for two minutes.
   ● How did it feel to be in the other position? Why?

3 What situations do you know that are somehow like this one with Jerry and Sandra?

Example 4

Why bother with this?
- it could help you look ahead to a situation in school where someone might have a narrow view of you
- it can give you a chance to think about how you might handle similar situations

The situation:

Tony is talking with his form tutor about the five options he wants to take in the fourth year

- He does well at *Geography* and knows he would like to carry it on next year
- He's getting on alright with *French*, so will probably decide to keep trying in that
- In *Art and Design* he would like to do more of the photography and other things he's started

That leaves *two more* to choose

Tony has met some of his Dad's friends who work in the hotel trade and get to travel quite a lot – he feels it's a line of work he would enjoy too. So he decides to do *Home Economics* and thinks he'll carry on a *General Science* lesson too.

But his form tutor says:

'Well there aren't many boys in Home Economics – do you think you'll like it? You're good at Physics and Chemistry – they're useful too'

---

1 Decide in groups of four:
   - What could Tony say?
   - What do you think would be the consequence of each of your suggestions?

write your ideas here:

2 What other situations do you know where someone thinks you won't do something 'because not many boys do'?

Example 5

Aim
– to consider an event where someone is saying how 'men' behave

The situation:

John has been to his usual Wednesday evening football training. After the session is over he goes to the pub with his mates (old school friends). Most of them order pints, but John feels very thirsty and wants something he can drink fast without affecting how he feels when he meets his girlfriend at 8:30.

He has seen some of his mates call people 'cissy' and 'wet' if they order any soft drinks...

1 What can John do?

He decides to order a 'Saint Clements' (a mixed orange juice and bitter lemon).

Bob (a tough goalie in the team) turns to John and says 'Not man enough for a pint?'

2 If you were John, what would you say to Bob?

6
Issues for teachers and pupils
Gill Venn

Introduction

The implementation of a pastoral curriculum containing components which focus on gender work has numerous implications for the practising teacher. This chapter aims to focus on some of the implications highlighted by a small-scale research project and also on the perceptions of pupils experiencing the activities.

Many teachers, when faced with presenting gender issues as part of a tutorial programme, consider using activity-based group work. The viewpoints of pupils and teachers outlined within this chapter are those of groups who have experienced gender-related activities within the context of an *Active Tutorial Work*[1] programme which incorporates such group work.

First this chapter outlines the original research, discussing the theoretical issues raised and those relating to practical implementation in the classroom. Second, it discusses the implications for teachers in more detail. Pupils' responses to the activities are investigated and finally, the implications for INSET are cited.

The original research

The original concern which initiated the first phase of the research was that the pastoral system in an all-boys school was dependent upon crisis-based management. Active Tutorial Work (ATW) was suggested as a possible solution to this problem and a pilot group was set up to follow the first year programme, providing the sample for the study. Gender-specific activities were undertaken with this group and although these did not form part of the original report, they will be referred to in this chapter. This initial group had no previous experience of ATW, but they had been following an anti-sexist course as part of the mainstream curriculum offer. A follow-up study was conducted in a mixed school with a comparable group of first-year pupils who had been following a tutorial package, but had no experience of gender-related activities.

Although the original study focussed on one particular ATW package, I feel that the findings may well be of interest to any teacher considering using such methodology when approaching gender-related activities. A theoretical examination of the aims, content and processes involved in the programme led me to question its political basis and to believe that it was about control – social control in a progressive package. It appeared that ATW was advocating progressive methods for non-progressive ends. Approaches such as group work were recommended in order to facilitate the growth of the group – but growth towards what ends? The research highlighted that the ATW package was more content than process based and that the content was largely about encouraging pupils to adapt and conform to the social norms of the school. It was consistently the pupils who were perceived as the problem, the school and the structure never being questioned. Once these theoretical issues had been raised, I embarked upon observing the group and interviewing pupils and staff.

Teaching approaches and common elements of process advocated by the programme were examined. As noted in the theoretical examination, by description they often appeared to be progressive and to facilitate 'active' learning; on observation they were mostly about pupil control. Each session observed was heavily teacher-directed in terms of activities, management, atmosphere and movement of pupils. The use of the circle proved to be a vehicle for providing structure to the sessions, yet it did not, in practice, place all the participants on equal status. The circle appeared to be conducive to whole group discussion, but an analysis of this activity showed that discussions were initiated by the teacher and participated in by the same small group of pupils each session. Developmental group work as prescribed by Button[2] was observed. Here again, teacher intervention was considerable. The agenda for discussion was set up by the programme, the groups decided by the teacher and the ensuing 'conversations' felt to be of little value by the pupils themselves. Indeed an investigation into small group work showed the opinion that the choice of partner proved problematic for the pupils, although this was not recognised by the course book. In addition, developmental group work was perceived by the teachers and pupils involved as being developmental in terms of the pupils being more successful at keeping on task after a period of involvement with the programme. There was no mention of continuity between sessions or of skills being developed.

Role play activities were also dictated by the programme and might be analysed as examples of attempts at behaviour/attitude modification. The

110

response by the pupils was to present stereotypical images of the characters involved and there was no follow-up discussion of the 'plays'.

The pupils were unable to state why they felt that ATW was included on their timetable. They were limited in their expression of how they felt it was of any benefit to them or to their progress elsewhere in the curriculum. They perceived it as being totally separate from the rest of the subject areas. When the subject teachers were interviewed, they too expressed the opinion that there was little or no transfer of learning takng place into their subject areas. The lack of transfer of learning was perhaps not surprising given the pupils' perception of the programme as being an entirely separate entity from the rest of the curriculum. I believe that this point is crucial. Marland[3] and Bethell[4] both argue that in order for the pastoral elements to be successful, it should form an integral part of the whole curriculum and that it should be concerned with the 'total welfare' of the child.

The issues raised by the research may appear quite negative and therefore controversial. It could indeed be argued that they are specific to one curriculum package that was offered in one school. However, I feel that they may be viewed more generally as the pitfalls to be avoided when groups of teachers or individuals are preparing materials and activities to use with pupils. In the following section, these and other implications for teachers will be explored.

Implications for teachers

This section aims to discuss the implications for teachers who are considering incorporating gender-related activities into their pastoral programmes. It will draw upon issues raised in the previous section, but only in terms of aims and methodology.

The issues explored here are closely interrelated. Each aspect has implications for INSET which will be summarised at the end of the section.

School policy

As with any policy, there are potential problems for a school in translating its gender policy into practice. The notion of a whole-school commitment to such a policy is often idealistic. Presuming that such a policy exists, are pupils made overtly aware of it? If so, how? These questions have direct implications for any gender work envisaged for pupils. What takes place in the tutorial group may or may not be reinforced by the pupils' general experience of school. Work undertaken and issues explored with pupils during such activities may be negated by simple things such as boys always being first on registers, separate sports in PE lessons and the distinct lack of women in positions of authority within the school's hierarchy. It is therefore important to take the position of whole-school policy into account when planning gender-related activities.

Working in teams

Whether or not the whole-school policy is successfully being translated into working practice may often depend upon individual teachers' attitudes within the institution. Colleagues often feel more at ease expressing their opinions in smaller groups rather than during whole-school debate. Their attitudes may often have a direct effect on the practice of working in teams on which many pastoral systems rely.

Gaining consensus on aims and objectives is obviously important and preferable when devising new courses and materials in terms of implementation. But is achieving consensus imperative? I would suggest that genuine consensus is rarely achieved and that this has implications for the role and skill of the team leader. The ability to encourage and support individuals and to deal with possible conflict is paramount. The ability to disseminate good practice is also useful. Even teachers who are overtly or covertly opposed to introducing gender issues into the curriculum will often be persuaded to try out new materials and methods when presented with examples of good practice.

If teams are presented with an initial flexible package of aims and objectives, with a few examples of potentially successful activities, the group can then discuss, from a more concrete basis, the way in which they want to develop and implement their programme for their pupils. This is important. Presenting reluctant teachers with a rigid, inflexible course which they, in turn, are expected to present to children will often be counter-productive. If teachers have been given the opportunity to discuss their opinions, express their doubts and contribute to the final package, they might be more inclined to present the work with the professional enthusiasm required for successful implementation. It will also be useful to acknowledge that some teachers who feel at ease with subject matter, might not feel so confident about suggested approaches.

Employing 'active' methodology

In recent years there have been a number of moves towards more 'active' learning in many aspects of the curriculum. Examples can be found in various initiatives; the negotiated curriculum, communicative approaches in Modern Languages, experiential learning, the use of Socratic discussion techniques, all of which encourage the pupils to taken an active part in the learning process rather than passively 'receiving' knowledge. Yet many teachers still feel more at ease with more didactic approaches. It is perhaps important to recognise this preference. Such teachers may already feel uneasy about the subject matter. Insisting that they then employ active methodology may add to their sense of vulnerability.

The previous section outlined some of the pitfalls to be wary of when adopting active methodology. One of the major recommendations of the research was that *all* teachers who are expected to use this form of approach need a major period of INSET to familiarise themselves with the suggested methods and to be afforded the opportunity of experiencing the activities themselves. One INSET day allocated to such 'training' is useful, but often inadequate. Teachers benefit greatly from being introduced to the approaches over a period of time and having plenty of opportunities for follow-up discussions on how they perceive it in terms of worth and ease.

Several suggestions for positive inclusion of 'active' methods arose from the research.

1 *The circle* as a vehicle for discussion only works – in terms of equality for all participants – if careful attention is paid to eliciting responses and contributions from everyone present. Whole group discussion needs to be very carefully structured by the teacher or leader in order for this to feel comfortable and worthwhile to the participants.
2 *Pair work* is often perceived as problematic by the pupils in terms of partner choice. This will be explored more thoroughly in the next section, but it is useful perhaps for teachers to recognise the area as being potentially problematic for pupils.
3 *Role plays.* Regardless of careful preparation and planning of activities which lead up to role play situations, be prepared to be presented with stereotypical images. Then use these images as a starting point for discussion. Follow-up discussions of role plays are as useful as the 'playing' itself and it is therefore important to allow sufficient time for unrushed debate.

If the 'team' opt to include elements of 'active' learning in their programmes, ideally each member should feel reasonably familiar with the approaches and supported by other members of the group.

Implications for INSET

Each of the issues outlined above raises implications for INSET. INSET for this type of work should be ongoing rather than a one day 'let's get acquainted with the programme' course. Ongoing INSET offers support and development both for individuals involved and for the programme itself.

School policy should evolve through the involvement of the whole staff in discussion and debate; its implementation being perceived as the responsibility of every member of staff. Equally, gender awareness should not be seen as a 'bolt on' but as integral to the whole school curriculum.

Working in teams and employing 'active' methodology also need a fairly long-term experiential approach and continual support for teachers. Staff should feel safe to express their opinions/doubts/optimism about the programme. Teams will discover their own set of pitfalls with both subject matter and methodology. These should be recognised, discussed and, where possible, rectifying suggestions made and tried out. Team leaders should also be provided with in-service training concerning the management of conflict.

Awareness of pupils' responses to the activities is explored in the following section, but it is perhaps useful to mention it here. Where possible, it is ideal for staff to have some time to elicit the pupils' perceptions of the course. This can be undertaken in whole groups and incorporated into the actual programme. Or a smaller number of pupils can be selected and 'interviewed'. This is often useful in determining what children perceive as positive aspects of the course, or problem areas. Such discussions may form a valid part of an on-going INSET package.

Pupils' responses to the activities

Teachers may feel very clear about the aims of the course as they perceive them and try to be aware of the 'messages' that are being transmitted to pupils. Yet it is perhaps useful to recognise that these 'messages' may not always be decoded by the pupils in the ways in which teachers anticipate.

As previously explained, two groups of first-year pupils were chosen to participate in the research. The first group were in an all-boys school, the follow-up group in a mixed school. The research raised issues for pupils which fell roughly into two categories: their reactions to the teaching approaches used and their perceptions of the subject content.

Pupils' responses to the approaches used

The teaching approaches used for the activities were similar in both the single sex and mixed schools and these produced and raised common issues for the pupils. Potentially problematic areas for teachers when adopting active approaches have already been explored. It is therefore perhaps interesting to also note the pupils' responses to these approaches.

Whole group discussion

Both groups of pupils equated sitting in a circle with whole-group discussion. Observations of the group of boys showed clearly that the same small group volunteered information, with the rest of the group remaining silent, appearing to listen. In the second, mixed group, most of the pupils participated, with the same small group each time remaining silent. Several pupils belonging to this second 'silent' group expressed fear at talking in large group situations. There was an equal number of boys and girls who expressed the fear. When one of the pupils was asked why he rarely spoke in whole group discussions, he replied,

I dunno, Miss. I get a bit scared. It's Ok. I don't mind listening.

It is perhaps interesting to note that in each of the sessions observed with the mixed group, on entry to the classroom, the pupils sat in separate gender groups. The quite common practice of playing games to 'shuffle' positions within the circle may make the teacher feel happier that the pupils are now no longer segregated by sex or that they might concentrate better now that potentially distracting friendship groups have been broken up, but this can cause problems for the pupils. Several expressed concern that, far from being able to work better when segregated from their friends, their concentration was disturbed by distractions caused by their new 'neighbour'. One girl expressed her concern:

Sitting around in a circle is good for talking and that – and I enjoy the swapping game, but I don't like it when I have to sit next to...'cos he keeps talking all the time and I can't think about what's going on.

Many teachers opt for a format which favours a whole-group introduction, then breaking down into small groups or pairs for discussion, with a return to the circle to 'share' ideas. Pupils' perceptions of small group activities will now be examined.

Small group and pair work

The majority of pupils interviewed appeared to hold strong feelings about working in small groups with other children. Teachers either allow freedom of choice of partners or dictate the groupings. When working with the mixed group I deliberately placed the pupils in mixed sex pairings as far as possible. None of the pupils interviewed felt threatened by this, although several expressed surprise that they had worked so well together. Even when the teacher feels that (s)he has allowed the pupils to make their own choice of partner, the pupils do not necessarily view it in the same way. The person they would choose to work with may be working with someone else, so although their freedom of choice has not been removed by the teacher, the pupil is never-the-less left with a restricted choice in their view.

> ME: *Who did you work with on Wednesday?*
> PM: *Afsha*
> ME: *Did you choose to work with Afsha?*
> PM: *Had no choice. I was gonna work with Jason, but Jason was working with Wayne so I worked with Afsha.*

A number of pupils expressed a very clear idea of who, in the class, they could work with and equally with whom they became distracted. A large number said they preferred working with pupils outside their immediate friendship groups as they found it easier to remain on task with friendship distractions removed.

> WB: *I work with Simon now.*
> ME: *And how is that working out?*
> WB: *It's good. Better than working with Curtis and that lot.*
> WB: *How did you come to start working with Simon?*
> ME: *I was going to the back to work with Curtis and I thought, 'I'll sit with Simon for a bit and see what happens.' And it was alright. I thought he was a good worker and now I've started working better.*
> ME: *Do you prefer the teacher to tell you who to work with or do you prefer to choose?*
> WB: *I prefer to choose.*

The fact that pupils find partner choice potentially problematic and that the pupils themselves often have quite clear notions about who they can and cannot work with, might suggest that the teacher needs to discuss the formation of small groups with the pupils themselves. This might enable full advantage to be taken of this form of classroom organisation.

Pupils' perceptions of subject content
Many of the pupils talked about the activities in terms of games. This was particularly true of the boys. Each boy interviewed talked about playing games. However, a number of the girls referred to the activities as work – one even likened them to tests;

> It was sort of like a test, but we were talking about what we thought and most lessons we don't do that.

The pupils' perceptions of the activities as either games or work will depend on their experience of other subjects and activities within the rest of the curriculum. This should perhaps be recognised if one is aiming for some form of transfer of learning to take place. If the pupil perceives the activities and subject content as being totally separate from the rest of her/his school experience, (s)he is perhaps less likely to take experiences gained into other areas. It could be argued that this issue of links with other subjects relates back to the notion of whole-school policy. There is perhaps little point if the pupils are expressing anti-sexist attitudes within your sessions, then walking out into the corridor and making sexist jokes or comments.

As mentioned earlier, I occasionally found it hard to differentiate between genuine responses from pupils and those which I felt they thought I wanted to hear. This was particularly true when interviewing the pupils in the all-boys school about the activities, as they had been undergoing an anti-sexist course as part of their mainstream curriculum. I found that it was more enlightening to eavesdrop on small group discussions and to listen carefully to the comments pupils were making to each other as they left the room. These generally felt more 'raw' and presented me with material that I could then work on with the pupils in the following sessions. At the end of a session where the pupils had been asked to choose which activities/actions had been undertaken by either a girl or boy twin,[5] Joanne rounded angrily on Michelle as they were leaving the room:

> *You were dead wrong for saying that Diana had to do the ironing 'cos she had to learn how to do things like that for when she got married!*

Despite the approaches being similar in both institutions, the findings showed significant differences in the pupils' perceptions of the subject content.

The research showed that an inherent danger of following a programme specifically centred on gender work in a single sex school, is that the pupils frequently express views that they perceive will fulfil the teacher's expectations. This is in stark contrast to the findings in a mixed school. Here there is scope for genuine interaction, debate and learning as pupils are placed in a position where they are asked to address the issues with members of the opposite sex. As previously stated, pupils expressed their surprise at how well they had worked with members of the opposite sex and commented that this had been the first time that they had been afforded the opportunity of doing so. There was evidence that attitudes had been challenged and in some cases changed. An example of this was noted during small group work where pupils were discussing how girls are often perceived as being 'good' and boys are often labelled as 'bad'. The children began by accepting this hypothethis, but through the process of discussion and argument they began to present examples which disproved the theory and they also arrived at possible reasons why such theories exist.

The findings clearly illustrated the obvious obstacles associated with undertaking gender work in a single sex school, where opportunities for such natural debate as outlined above are not possible. However, this should not be seen as presenting an argument against inclusion of gender issues in such institutions. Rather, it should be recognised that in a single sex school, the teacher might be placed in the position of being the one person in the debate who is challenging the consensus. Clearly it is important for all teachers to be aware of their position when addressing gender issues, but this is of particular importance for those staff undertaking activities in a single sex school. The teacher must be prepared to be confronted with stereotypical views presented in a forceful manner. The research noted that a number of pupils responded to the activities in this manner. The teacher responded sympathetically to their ideas and preconceptions, whilst presenting the opposing view.

When considering the fact that the majority of pupils had difficulty in expressing the aims of the 'course', it is perhaps useful to recognise that until recently many pupils would be unable to express the aims of a lot of what they do in school. Just as Records of Achievement are beginning to encourage teachers to make the aims of subject courses more explicit to pupils, so perhaps should the aims of all PSE work, including gender-related activities be made more explicit. When pupils are presented with a set of clearly-defined aims concerning the activities they are experiencing, they appear to feel more secure with the work and generally become more actively involved with the sessions.

A group of pupils whose perceptions need to be recognised, understood and addressed when considering implementation of an anti-sexist programme, or indeed policy, is the Asian community within many schools. When pupils draw upon their culture in order to express opinions and values, the attitudes reflected may not be in accordance with those of the teacher leading the session, or indeed of the policy that the teacher is aiming to implement. A policy which, on one hand, recognises the importance of respecting other cultures, yet on the other strongly advocates challenging sexist notions may leave the individual teacher feeling unclear about her/his role when attempting gender-related activities. I feel that the key to this dilemma is respect. If the teacher, and indeed the school, present an understanding of culture and gender in a non-stereotypical way and aim to respect the individual experiences of pupils, offering an alternative view will not be seen as threatening or as overriding any one culture.

It would be rather optimistic to expect to change attitudes overnight. However, if the subject content and approaches decided upon are reinforced throughout the rest of the pupils' school experience, the opportunity of achieving progress might be more readily realised. It is important that gender work is undertaken within a framework of a working equal opportunities policy. LEA commitment to equal opportunities policies might aid their implementation, which in turn might ensure that gender issues are more clearly understood and more readily taken on by teachers and pupils. But LEA enforcement cannot and should not be the whole answer. Long-term INSET for staff and a whole-school commitment to gender issues across the curriculum are critical to successful implementation of activities which concentrate on issues of gender.

This chapter has raised a number of issues for teachers considering introducing gender work with their pupils. Finally, I would like to propose a number of questions which might be of some use at the planning stage, or when INSET programmes are being considered.

- *What am I aiming towards?*
- *How does the institution back up or negate these aims?*
- *Should I make my aims explicit to the pupils? If so, in what format?*
- *Are the activities I've devised/decided to use familiar to the pupils? Have they experience of such methodology elsewhere in the curriculum? If not, what implications does this have for the work I've planned?*
- *What are the implications of the planned work for INSET and the involvement of other staff?*
- *How, if at all, will I monitor pupil progress and their responses to the activities?*

*　*　*　*　*

References

1　Baldwin, J. and Wells, H. (1979) *Active Tutorial Work Books 1–5* (The Lancashire Project) Basil Blackwell.
2　Button, L. (1981) *Group Tutoring for the Form Tutor* Hodder and Stoughton.
3　Marland, M. (1974) *Pastoral Care* Heinemann.
4　Bethel, A. (1976) Who Cares? in *Teaching London Kids* No 8.
5　Pepper, B., Myers, K. and Coyle/Dawkins, R. (1984) *Sex Equality in the Pastoral Curriculum* ILEA Spencer Park Teachers' Centre.

Further reading

Victor, G. (1987) *In Search of a Pastoral Curriculum: An Exploration of Active Tutorial Work* M.Ed Dissertation, North East London Polytechnic (now Polytechnic of East London).

7
Combatting inequality – Combatting an isolated approach

Sue Askew and Carol Ross

Introduction

With the advent of the National Curriculum there is a stronger emphasis on achievement and subject areas throughout the whole of the child's schooling. It is vital to establish a pastoral context within this to ensure that every child benefits fully from the educational opportunities on offer. Promoting equal opportunities in terms of gender, race and class must be concerned with ensuring equal access to all children. National Curriculum documents state that the core and foundation subject areas do not make up the entire curriculum. They refer to wider issues such as health education, careers and equal opportunities, but leave it to Local Education Authorities and schools to decide on appropriate formats. But what is the best way to address these issues?

During the time we have worked in schools we have been involved in organising, planning and teaching PSE courses; more recently we have worked as Advisory Teachers in Equal Opportunities. A large part of this work has been in response to requests from teachers to develop an anti-sexist focus within PSE.

In the schools in which we have been involved the PSE course has usually been set up to fill gaps in the curriculum and/or to enhance personal and social development. The first has involved working on such topics as health education (including sex and drug education); careers education; specific social issues (such as abortion, AIDS and issues to do with racism and sexism). The second has involved working on, for example, communication skills, decision making, study skills and pupil collaboration, interaction and negotiation and individual autonomy.

In our experience PSE courses have often been developed as a response to specific needs which are perceived in the pupils. These needs are usually related to various behavioural problems, such as bullying and an inability to work co-operatively and to difficulties children are thought to have, such as difficulties in expressing themselves or problems with self-esteem.

In this chapter we focus on equal opportunities in terms of gender. We argue *against* the setting up of a *separate* 'pastoral curriculum' and that:

- social and personal educational issues are inseparable from gender and other issues of inequality;
- issues of inequality cannot be tackled as 'topic' areas within a separate PSE course;
- each subject area needs to be examined for bias and stereotypes;
- because the aims of PSE are centrally bound up with issues of inequality, a PSE course cannot solve problems which are essentially related to institutional inequality.

We argue for the following:

1 There should be a structure for pastoral care which operates on an Institutional level with the form tutor having a central role.
2 The pastoral teachers (form tutor, Head of Year, Head of House) should have a role which is concerned with mediating between the pupil, the institution and parents/the community in relation to pupil achievement. This would involve monitoring the progress of children and indentifying any particular issues in terms of gender, race and class which are affecting their achievement.
3 This should be a two-way process so that (i) the teacher helps the children to negotiate the institution (ii) problems pupils are having which relate to inequalities can be conveyed through formalised channels to be addressed on an institutional level.

The relationship between the aims of PSE and issues of inequality

Both the stated and underlying aims of PSE implicitly involve gender and issues of inequality. Many of the issues that PSE is concerned about (the individual and collective behaviour and attitudes of pupils) are fundamentally related to social position and power relationships.

To illustrate this point we will look at two main aims commonly stated for separate PSE courses:

1 To enhance group processes; including co-operation, collaboration and mutual respect.
2 To promote personal autonomy including awareness of choices and decision-making skills.

In themselves, of course, both aims are praiseworthy. We would all encourage considerate and positive interaction between children and want to see them make 'healthy' and enriching decisions about their lives. The motivation for a PSE course often stems from the observation that pupils are operating less successfully in these areas than might be hoped. However, to focus attention exclusively on changing the pupils' behaviour is to assume a deficit model of the individual and view their behaviour out of its social context. The context in which children are socialised ascribes them different behaviour and expectations for different roles in society.

In this society everyone has, in theory, equal access to opportunities. In reality, members of particular groups are constrained from being able to gain entry to high status positions in the economic sphere. These constraints may be practical, for example, lack of childcare facilities, or they may be to do with discrimination. They may also be related to particular ideas about members of social groups which relate to their ability, personality, characteristics and skills. Ideas about different social groups will both reflect their social position and also ensure their 'unsuitability' for different roles. For example, in terms of gender, the socialisation of women usually includes developing qualities which 'fit' them for caring and servicing roles. Qualities which are seen as enhancing this role include characteristics such as 'nurturing', 'supportiveness', and an empathetic nature. Other characteristics ascribed to women may be more negative. Notions of women as dependent, passive, over-emotional, bad at maths and science and irrational are, however, not inconsistent with women's social roles. In fact these ideas ensure that they are excluded from the male domain.

On the other hand, socialisation of men promotes contrasting characteristics such as independence, decisiveness, competitiveness, being mechanically minded and good at maths and science, being unemotional – qualities which support traditional 'male' occupations. These ideas result in a very narrow range of characteristics which are thought appropriate for each gender and prevent us reaching our full potential. Additionally these ideas result in women and men being valued in different ways. What is regarded as 'desirable' for one gender may not be for the other. Social institutions are often founded on such stereotyped ideas about social groups and, in turn, will be instrumental in disseminating them.

The position of people in terms of their class, race and gender carries with it different degrees of social and economic power. The socialisation and education of children relates to this. Class, race and gender affect how children are viewed and what is offered to them by the institution itself; children's own perceptions (their expectations, the skills and interests they develop). For example at the individual level girls may feel their talents and skills lean toward those subjects with 'human interest', such as social studies, English or home economics; they may feel incompetent or disinterested in scientific or mathematical subjects and they may find it difficult to recognise and assert their own needs. Boys may be very 'activity' oriented, preferring to make and do rather than read, write or discuss; they may be overly competitive and only able to work in an individualistic way; or caught up in an aggressive cycle of juxtapositioning for power and status. At the 'group' level boys may dominate teacher time and attention, classroom space and equipment and harass girls in the process; at the institutional level the curriculum may reflect bias in terms of language, images and content. Girls and boys may be channelled into different options and career choices.

Group dynamics and the choices and decisions made by individual children must not be seen out of context of the children's social position. This is an important consideration with regard to the aims of PSE. To ignore this is to assume that a classroom is an aggregate of individuals with all things essentially equal – rather than an aggregate of social groups with varying degrees of power in society. If these social divisions and the resultant inequalities are not recognised then the children's different realities cannot be taken into consideration. For example, if it not recognised that there is an expectation on girls to fulfil a supportive and empathetic role generally in society, they may assume this role in the group without anyone questioning it. Trying to teach 'decision making' as a skill out of context also assumes that children are all in an equal position and only lack the necessary practice. In reality children may not lack skills, but some choices may not be genuinely open to them because of social and economic factors.

Class, race and gender issues are indivisible from such concepts as collaboration, respect, autonomy and decision making. This may seem to lead to the argument that we should devise a PSE course which directly confronts issues of inequality. However we now go on to argue against this.

Problems with using a separate course of PSE to address equal opportunity issues

Schools we have worked in have tended to incorporate equal opportunity issues in their PSE courses in two rather different ways:

1 Through discussion within PSE about explicit issues such as 'roles in the home', images of girls and boys; bias in the media.
2 Through attempts to address 'implicit' issues as a means of 'intervening'

in the socialisation processes, eg assertiveness training for girls; personal communication skills for boys.

Explicit issues

We have worked on several units within PSE courses which have had as their main purpose the intention of raising the childrens' awareness. For example, in one unit pupils looked at 'roles in the home.' They explored such things as who did which jobs in the home; who spent most time doing housework; who did the most childcare and so on. In another unit we looked at images of girls and boys, including the clothes they wear; the toys they play with; their interests and hobbies, expectations for them and by them. A third unit explored sexism in the media by examining the way men and women are portrayed; stereotyped roles on TV, children's books and comics and so on.

These units on gender awareness were problematic for two main reasons: first, pointing out the stereotypes did not necessarily help the children to challenge them; second, it is not possible to talk about gender issues at that kind of theoretical level while ignoring the realities of gender behaviour and interaction taking place in the classroom itself. In our society we are continually surrounded by stereotyped gender images. These images are so commonplace that we often accept them as normal, but even more, as desirable. In fact there may be pressure to regard oneself or others as deviant if they don't conform. For example, notions about what is attractive in a woman are very precise. We are presented with images of a 'desirable' woman as slim, long-legged and attentive. Little girls are given long-haired, blue-eyed Sindy dolls to play with. By pointing out to children the image of a desirable women in this society we are merely confirming to them what they see to be true or even worse reinforcing it. To children most gender stereotypes are the norm; describing them does not make children critical of them. Additionally we observed that in discussion many children talked about themselves and their lives in stereotyped terms. For example, in a discussion about roles in the home, one boy insisted his mother did all the housework and cooking. However the teacher knew that his father was unemployed and, in fact, did most of the work at home, while his mother was out at work. It seemed to us that children have a great need to conform to their idea of what's normal and do not want to be different. Even though we had hoped to change their ideas of gender norms we found we could not do this by telling them these norms were 'wrong'.

The kinds of problems we have raised of doing explicit work on sexism are not exclusive to a PSE course; they may arise in any subject area where anti-sexist work is attempted. However, the more closely the issues are linked to a subject area and the more natural a context they arise in, the more children seem able to relate to and understand them. For this reason we believe that explicit Equal Opportunity issues are best explored with children *within* subject areas. For example, helping children to become critical readers in English lessons would include developing an awareness of bias and stereotypes in literature. In History, teachers would want to provide materials which showed the experiences and perspectives of a variety of people – in this way the contribution of women, for example, would become visible. However, the most natural context of all is following up issues as they arise, regardless of the subject area this occurs in.

Implicit issues

Some schools have identified the children's behaviour and relationships as the underlying gender issues with which they are concerned. This has become the focus for the PSE units. Some teachers found that they could not even begin to discuss the explicit issues they wanted to raise because of the general interaction between pupils, including bullying, teasing, competiveness and harassment.

The aim was to help the boys to be less competitive, collaborate more easily, take responsibility for themselves and others and behave more caringly generally. The aim for the girls was to help them to stand up for their rights; assert their own needs; make positive choices and build up their self-confidence. For the boys, situations were devised that were collaborative and interactive such as group tasks; visitors were invited in and the boys made responsible for them; games were played that developed listening skills; discussions were held about personal feelings and fears, for instance, times they had felt scared, times they were bullied. Girls were instructed in assertiveness techniques, practised decision-making skills through role play, formalised situations where they made positive statements about themselves and each other.

We attempted to monitor this work to see how far the goals were realised. For example, we observed boys in other situations and talked to their teachers to see if their ability to collaborate had improved. Although such monitoring was highly subjective, teachers felt that they knew the children in their classes well enough to be sensitive to changes in the pupils' way of negotiating situations and interacting with each other. Such monitoring was of a range of PSE classes, taught by different teachers over a considerable period of time. There was agreement that the PSE work was not achieving the goals set. We feel that there were various reasons why this should be so. Children's experiences in the PSE lessons were largely unrelated to their experiences in the rest of the school. They didn't extend the behaviour that was being promoted to other lessons. Sometimes this was because the context was so different, for example, in some lessons they were put in competitive situations and expected to work in individualistic ways. Teaching styles were sometimes authoritarian and didn't allow the children to take responsibility for their own behaviour or negotiate the situations.

Another problem we found with this approach was that what we were trying to do was out of a meaningful context. For girls the aim of helping them become more assertive didn't engage with their school situation. We now think that assertiveness training should be directly related to the actual situations in school in which it is meant to be applied – to teach the girls to stand up to the boys in maths lessons, assertion training must take place *in* the maths lesson, or at least directly address that situation. Getting boys to collaborate in the PSE lesson was a specific aim and the tasks devised were merely foils for this. However, within subject lessons there is the opportunity to collaborate over tasks which are meaningful in themselves. We believe that for skills to be transferable they must be developed in relation to a 'real' situation so that the children can try out the skills, see they can change outcomes and have the skills reinforced.

The difficulty with a planned curriculum of PSE is that the content of each lesson follows a set course. The result of this was that problems which children face in the classroom, on the playground and in the school generally were not discussed in the PSE lessons unless it happended to coincide with the topic of the day. For example, in one lesson on harassment 'trigger' drawings were prepared in the hope that these would enable children to bring their own experiences to the discussion. Although some children did talk about personal incidents, the discussions on the whole remained on a hypothetical plane. Because of the fact that the PSE lessons were covering a planned curriculum there wasn't the 'genuine' opportunity or encouragement for pupils to raise things as they happened. The lessons were *meant* to be structured in such a way that pupils could bring their own experiences to lessons. In fact we observed that this tight structuring itself only reinforced the reality that the teacher controlled the agenda for discussion. This meant that the teaching methodology often conflicted with the desired aims.

Teaching behavioural skills out of context gives rise to the related problem of children often being unable to see the point of what they are doing. We found the idea of a 'preventative' approach to bullying and other behaviour that causes concern essentially ineffective unless we were able to change the circumstances in which it occurred or could talk to pupils about incidents *when* they occurred and involved pupils in deciding solutions. In one particular class a lot of fighting took place at break times. The pupils decided it would be best dealt with by providing a space for them to play board games. This was arranged and the behaviour changed.

In school all the PSE aims ought to relate to enabling children to broaden their opportunities and develop their full academic potential. PSE work with the children would be about helping them negotiate the school system. We have argued that aims to do with collaborative skills should be taught within the context of meaningful tasks. We would further argue that aims such as decision making should be incorporated into school life, including helping children make real decisions directly relating to school; understanding and challenging unfair limitations on their choices.

PSE aims and institutional inequality

Promoting the aims of PSE in a meaningful way involves examining equality of opportunity at all levels in the institution. This entails looking at the intended curriculum, the structure and organisation of the school, teaching methods and discipline. The curriculum itself conveys bias which directs girls and boys along gender-related paths, through its language, content, the way subjects are seen as either girls' subjects or boys' subjects, and stereotypes in the learning materials. Aspects of the institution have very obvious implications for the way they influence children's attitudes, expectations, behaviour and the choices they make. Examples include the way in which the option choices are grouped and presented; the kinds of career counselling available; teachers as role models (who teaches which subjects). Some aspects are far more subtle but equally damaging because of the messages they give about social norms. Positions in the hierarchy; the way the staff work together; values and ethos of the school; status, roles and make up of non-teaching staff, all give powerful statements. Teachers have cited many examples:

> *This is a girls' school and yet every single Head of Department, except for Home Economics and Business Studies, is a man.*
>
> *There seems to be a strong hierarchical structure with everyone competing for promotion. In order to rise up through the ranks you get further removed from your colleagues down there. This structure doesn't allow for real collaboration among staff.*

Modes of discipline are another aspect of the way schools operate which convey strong messages about power relationships. Authoritarian methods may involve a model of 'might is right' and involve explicit or implicit threats of physical force, loud shouting and a general show of aggressive power. Many teachers we talked to commented on how this set a bad 'example' to the pupils:

> *How can you expect the pupils to not bully each other when their Head of Year is just a big bully himself. He pushes the kids around and is always shouting at them.*
>
> *In our school discipline is maintained through threats. One boy told me the other day that his teacher said he'd 'pin' him up against the wall if he didn't shut up.*

We have argued that issues of inequality such as sexism are inseparable from the aims of PSE and that:

- the links between inequality and the aims of PSE are seldom made explicit.
- PSE aims cannot be taken out of the context of the institution. Ensuring equality of opportunity through pastoral care must be concerned with all aspects of institutional life.
- the establishment of a separate course of PSE can compound inequality by marginalising the issues and placing the onus for change on the victims of inequality.

The next section develops a model which sees a strong role for the form tutor and Head of Year as mediators between the pupils and the institution. It also gives workshop ideas to help facilitate staff discussion about some relevant issues.

Role of the pastoral staff

Clearly the form tutor has an important role to play in the pastoral care of children and this must involve taking on Equal Opportunity issues. We see the form tutor's function as being to oversee the progress of pupils; recognise their particular needs and look at these in relation to the rest of the school: How is the pupil achieving across the curriculum? What expectations and perceptions do teachers have of the pupil? What kinds of choices are being made? How is school experience generally affecting the pupil? What are the pupils' opportunities generally and how do these relate to issues such as gender? These concerns must be appraised in relation to Equal Opportunity aims. If the form tutor feels that, for example, too many girls in the form are consistently underachieving in Science, then it's necessary to explore the ways the Institution may be perpetuating social inequality and deliberate strategies need to be discussed. In this model of form tutoring, institutional changes would need to be made to allow the teacher timetabled time to visit their form's subject classes; talk to their teachers or withdraw children for individual discussions; liaise with the Head of Year, subject teachers, Equal Opportunities working party etc. This would be in addition to timetabled form period time. These times could be used to look at a variety of factors as they affect the pupil's achievement. Example of such uses include:

1 Identify specific problems as they arise through observation and discussion. For example, in one secondary school each form tutor had a day

each half-term to 'follow' their form through different lessons. By making this a different day each half-term over the course of the year the form teacher was able to observe their form in all lessons. A full-time supply teacher was allocated to provide cover to enable this to happen. A range of issues arose out of the observation. For example, several form teachers noted that the girls were marginalised in terms of teacher attention by keeping a 'low profile'. This was discussed in a Year meeting and it was agreed that an observation schedule should be drawn up for other form teachers and subject teachers to evaluate the situation.

These issues were then addressed with pupils during form period time. This gave real meaning to form time because pupils were aware that their form tutors had a better overview of their total school experience and the things discussed during form time were important to them.

2   Work with pupils on a group basis on issues *as they arise* (as opposed to a planned curriculum). This would involve helping pupils negotiate problems and develop coping strategies. This may take a variety of directions. For example, it may involve bringing the issue to the attention of the pupils so that they can be involved in negotiating the solution. It may involve discussion/exploration with pupils in form time to help them decide how to deal with the problem.

3   Together with the Head of Year/House, liaise with parents, both listening to and communicating about the pupils' progress. For example, in one school the Head of Year and Form Tutor hold twice-yearly meetings with parents, instead of the traditional parents' evenings where parents have a few minutes with all the subject teachers. The work from all departments is accumulated and displayed for parents to look at. The informality of the evening, together with the close connection developed between the form teacher, pupil and parents, makes the school much more accessible to the parents. It also means that parents' involvement and co-operation can be much stronger in terms of evaluating pupils' needs, progress and behaviour.

4   Talk to pupils about the choices they make. This may be concerned with such things as option choices. It's particularly important in relation to equal opportunities that the form tutor has an understanding of the influences on pupil decision making. For example, in one form there was a girl who was particularly able in Physics. She had not chosen Physics as an 'additional' Science and it was discovered that she was worried she would be the only girl in the class. There were in fact three other girls who had opted for Physics in another form and she subsequently decided to do it after all. The following year at option time a woman engineer came into school to talk to all the girls about careers for women in Science.

5   Relay information and observations back to the Head of Year so that Institutional changes can be made. Networks have to be set up so that there are formalised channels of communication between the form tutor/

subject teachers, Head of Year and senior teachers. For example, in one school it was decided to focus on a couple of specific equal opportunity issues each term. At the beginning of the term strategies and goals were set by each year team. At the end of each term progress was evaluated and new strategies put forward. These were 'fed' back to the equal opportunity working party and to Departmental meetings.

In order for the form tutors to be effective in their role it is vital that in-service training programmes are built in which incorporate looking at sexism and other areas of inequality.

Pastoral aims must be in the context of furthering children's achievement in school. Combatting sexism and other inequalities is about ensuring that children achieve their full potential so that factors such as gender don't impose limits on the opportunities for their development. Good pastoral work and anti-sexist work are in this sense one and the same.

In summary, the model which has been discussed requires effective communication throughout the whole school system, and particularly in the pastoral network. Figure 7.1 summarises this process.

The means by which such an effective network is likely to be developed will include in-service work and active workshops, in which staff can identify and address issues. Figures 7.2–7.5 are examples of stimulus material we have used in order to start off discussion on the issues raised in this chapter. Such starters to discussion can then lead into a structured examination of how your school functions, followed by clear proposals for change.

Figure 7.1 Creating a pastoral network for promoting equal opportunities.

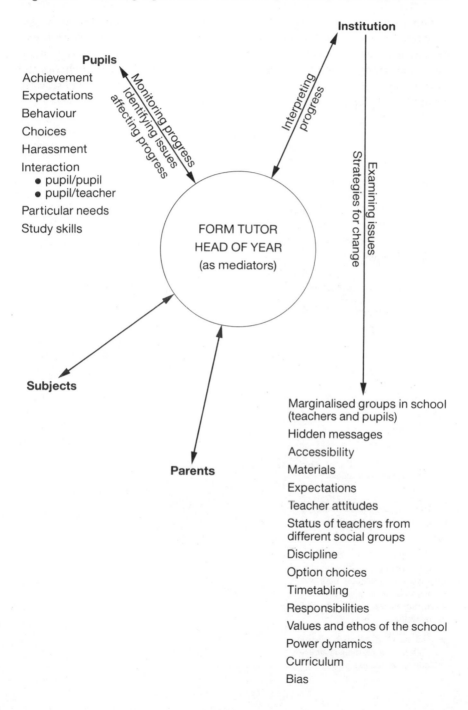

Institution

Pupils

Achievement
Expectations
Behaviour
Choices
Harassment
Interaction
  • pupil/pupil
  • pupil/teacher
Particular needs
Study skills

Monitoring progress
Identifying issues
affecting progress

Interpreting progress

Examining issues
Strategies for change

FORM TUTOR
HEAD OF YEAR
(as mediators)

Subjects

Parents

Marginalised groups in school
(teachers and pupils)

Hidden messages

Accessibility

Materials

Expectations

Teacher attitudes

Status of teachers from
different social groups

Discipline

Option choices

Timetabling

Responsibilities

Values and ethos of the school

Power dynamics

Curriculum

Bias

Figure 7.2 Workshop – General Issues

This workshop has been used to begin to introduce some relevant issues. Participants began by individually filling in the question sheet, then forming small groups to discuss each statement, particularly those over which there was strong agreement or disagreement. They were asked to choose the statement/s which, as a group, they felt most strongly about. These were brought back for a whole group discussion.

	STRONGLY AGREE	AGREE	DON'T KNOW	DISAGREE	STRONGLY DISAGREE
1 Issues of inequality are essentially attitudinal and can be set right through a PSE course which stresses awareness on the part of the children.					
2 A course on PSE can make a difference to inequalities on an institutional level.					
3 A PSE course can get to grips with the equal opportunities needs of children in terms of their achievement.					
4 A PSE course is taking time and attention away from promoting equal opportunities in each subject area.					
5 The problems of pupil behaviour which a PSE course seeks to address are related to issues of class, race and gender.					
6 PSE is set up as a 'plaster' to cover the ills of institutional inequality.					
7 PSE assumes a deficit model of children, who it sets out to 'cure'.					
8 PSE should not be a course in itself but an approach throughout the school to ensure that aims related to personal development are within a context of achievement.					
9 Having a PSE course is worse than not having anything at all in relation to racism and sexism.					

Figure 7.3 Workshop on Anti-Sexist Aims

In pairs
a) Consider the possible aims below. Rewrite them, add
    your own, discard, etc until you are left with *nine*
    reasonable statements.

b) Prioritise the statements in a 'diamond nine'.

```
          1
        2   2
      3   3   3
        4   4
          5
```

In small groups Compare priorities, discuss and try to reach a consensus.
Whole group Begin to think of ways in which the prioritised aims relate to
the aims of PSE.

To help boys empathise with others/ to help girls assert their own needs	To expore ways in which people are sex-role stereotyped in conjunction with race and class stereotypes.
To change children's sexist attitudes	To look at stereotyped images in the media (books, films, TV, posters, etc)
To reappraise the option choices pupils are making and develop positive interventions	To look at messages about power relationships implicit within modes of discipline in the school
To look at the position of staff in the school in terms of what they teach, and their position in the hierarchy in relation to their gender and race	Write your own
To develop effective strategies for dealing with sexual harassment	

Figure 7.4 Workshop on form tutoring to promote equal opportunities

The following statements were made by form tutors describing situations which arose that they felt had implications for equal opportunities.

In small groups, teachers in the workshops chose statements most relevant to their own situation, discussed the underlying issues involved and devised possible strategies.

A girl in my form has always been very keen and able in physics. Now I hear she wants to drop it. I'm worried that this might be because there are only three girls in her class.

Three girls in my form are being harassed at break-time by some older boys. I tried talking to them. That did nothing, so I reported this to their head of year, but it's still going on.

I go in to support my form's maths lessons and I've noticed that the girls always sit at the back and don't get much attention.

I'm generally concerned about the kinds of discipline procedures used on my form. I feel it's giving them an aggressive model, especially the boys. I think it's reinforcing their idea that 'might is right'.

A parent of a girl in my form visited me last week and said she was worried that her daughter's CDT teacher didn't take her seriously because she is a girl.

Figure 7.5 Workshop on creating networks for promoting equal opportunities.

This workshop was used as a focus for thinking about how to develop communication channels between the form tutor/head of year and the rest of the school and parents.

1 The statements were completed individually.
2 The results were compared in small groups.
3 The groups shared their ideas and tried to reach a consensus on action.

a The best way for the form tutor to monitor pupil progress in relation to equal opportunities would be _____

_____

b The head of year's role in relation to monitoring progress is

_____

_____

c The form tutor can best identify issues affecting progress by

_____

_____

d The best channels for relaying observations about pupils are

_____

_____

e Issues arising from tutor observations could be fed into

_____

_____

f The form tutor's role in relation to achievement and subject teachers is

_____

_____

g Pupils could be best encouraged to relate equal opportunity issues to form tutors by_____

_____

h Parents should be involved in the process of identifying equal opportunity needs by_____

_____

Published classroom resources for addressing gender

Sue Adler

This is not a complete listing. It was compiled to give readers access to some of the classroom resources for addressing gender themes. Some titles are presently out of print from publishers, so readers would need to access copies through libraries and inter-library loan.

Askew, Sue and Carol Ross
Anti-sexist Work with Boys.
Equal Opportunities Commission, 1984

A report of the 'Skills For Living' course for first and second year boys developed in Hackney Downs School. It includes numerous worksheets and classroom materials.

The B Team
Boys Work Posters.
The B Team, c/o BCM B Team, London WC1N 3XX

Six A3 black and white posters plus notes. Designed to help start discussion of masculinity with boys and young men. The images chosen were the result of discussions and photo sessions with young men in a youth project.

Carter, Anne; Magee, Frances; Mapp, Les; Myers, Kate; Rospigliosi, Ross and Watkins, Chris
Equal Opportunities: What's In It For Boys?
ILEA/ Schools Council, 1983
Whyld Publishing Co-op, 1986
Moorland House, Caistor, Lincs LN7 6SF

A pack of materials for teachers, including activities for work with teachers and activities for use in the classroom.

136

The Clarity Collective
Taught not Caught: Strategies for Sex Education;
British edition edited by Hilary Dixon and Gill Mullinar.
Learning Development Aids 1985
ISBN 0 905 114 159

'We are convinced that the planning and presentation of sex education should encompass the opportunity for exploration of values and attitudes and the growth of skills necessary to build relationships, communicate and make decisions' (introduction)

Development Education Centre
Hidden Messages: Activities for Exploring Bias
(Development Education in the Primary School Book 2)
Birmingham, Development Education Centre
ISBN 0 9506619 9 6

A framework for teachers to examine their own ideas, and a series of classroom suggestions and exercises to help children recognize different kinds of bias. Practical and full of straight-forward ideas for working on in a complex (and essential) area.

Girls and Occupational Choice Project
Hidden Messages: an Equal Opportunities Teaching Pack.
GAOC and Blackwell, 1989.
ISBN 0 631 901396

The curriculum materials in this spiral bound package are one product of the work of the GAOC project, which focussed on the years before option choice. It is a flexible resource which can be used in sections or as individual worksheets, across the curriculum.

Hughes, Nym, Yvonne Johnson and Yvette Perreault
Stepping Out of Line: a Workbook on Lesbianism and Feminism.
Vancouver, Gang Press. 1984.
ISBN 0 88974 016 X

Provides a workshop script (with practical details on running it) and stories from many lesbians. Written for use with adults – but there is much in it accessible to 15+ in school and colleges.

Leigh, M.
Messages: A Booklet for Use in Workshops and Seminars Concerned with Sexism and the Development of Non-Sexist Work with Young People.
World Council Of Churches, 1984
Material developed from a Christian perspective.

New Grapevine
The Grapevine Game: Sex and Sexuality.
New Grapevine 1984

> A board game with pamphlet. This is not a game with winners and losers, but a valuable learning package. Deals with many aspects of the subject including sex roles, harassment, sexual identity, contraception. It avoids making assumptions about players' knowledge, or their sexual orientation.

Newsreel Collective
True Romance etc: a Booklet to Accompany the Film.
Newsreel Collective, 1985

> Intended to stimulate discussion. It can be used without the film – it is a short and pithy look at the hazards and hassles of relationships.

Szirom, Tricia and Sue Dyson
Greater Expectations: a Source Book for Working with Girls and Young Women; British edition edited by Hazel Slavin.
Learning Development Aids, 1986.
ISBN 0 905 114191

> A resource to raise awareness on gender, it is full of activities and strategies to help groups and individuals learn more about women in society. Includes worksheets which are copyright free. Particularly useful for 14+, youth and adult groups (of boys and men as well as girls and women.)

Thompson, Doug Cooper
As Boys become Men: Learning New Male Roles. A Curriculum for Exploring Male Role Stereotyping.
New York, Irvington 1985.
ISBN 0 8290 1591 4

> Provides a structure for examining masculinity, looking at the male student and male roles as an issue in gender studies and gender equality. Useful and usable worksheets on work, language, media, emotions etc.

Thompson, Jane
All Right For Some: The Problem of Sexism
Hutchinson, 1986
ISBN 0 09 164721 5

> Lively and varied design – it uses comic strip, photos, games. A jokey but never trivialising book on sex roles and sexual oppression, with lots of activities – and lots of teenager appeal.

Walker, Dorothy
Gender Equality: an Effective Resource for Today's Classroom
Learning Development Aids, 1986
publisher's ref no. LD766

> A spiral bound pack of materials to raise primary school children's awareness of gender bias and help confront and challenge it. Practical, tried and tested extensively, and recommended for secondary schools too.

SECTION THREE
WORKING WITH
INDIVIDUALS AND FAMILIES:
THE GENDER ELEMENTS

Introduction

The two chapters in this section focus on the gender issues in working with individual pupils and families. Both of these areas have received little attention in writings related to schools and this is one reason for the inclusion of this section. Other reasons are that the writers believe that the biggest impact of schools is through individual relationships and that the family influences an individual more than the school. The family and individual relationships in school are highly influential in shaping gender images and gender expectations: they will contribute to a young person's gender identity.

In the first chapter of this section, Colleen McLaughlin examines the planned and unplanned interactions between teachers and individual pupils. These interactions can be powerful in shaping notions of what is appropriate for the different sexes; she argues that teachers need to be aware of their potential influence. Guidance is an important aspect of pastoral care for individual careers through school can be influenced.

The second chapter of this section deals with working with families. Patsy Wagner demonstrates that our pupils come from homes and families of many and varied arrangements. She argues that schools often misrepresent the complexity of these arrangements in the procedures and practices they adopt and thereby deny the reality of the pupil's experience. Some pupils and parents can be alienated. These same homes are places in which children learn certain roles which relate to areas of power in the family *viz* economic, emotional and social power. These roles also relate to gender. Gender roles restrict the options a person has merely on the basis of what sex they happen to be, thus they distort the development of both women and men and prevent them from having as much fulfilment as they might otherwise have.

Gender roles also have insidious effects on the mental health and physical well-being of both women and men, eg women are more likely than men to become mentally ill if they marry and men are more likely than women to develop stress-related illnesses such as ulcers and heart attacks. Men are also more likely to die shortly after retirement (when that occurs at 65).

Schools need to be aware of these issues so that they are better able to ensure that pupils of both sexes have full access to the curriculum and so that they are welcoming to pupils, parents and families. Schools also need to think carefully about the most effective procedures and practices for engaging and working with parents and families, eg practices of communication and meetings with parents.

Both chapters examine the respective issues and offer practical guidance to tutors, teachers and pastoral teams on dealing with individual pupils and on working out how to engage with families. Individual teachers can act immediately on the issues raised in these chapters for they can review and change their practice unaided. Awareness of the self, processes around the formation of gender identity and the interaction with families can also be developed.

8
Working with individual pupils

Colleen McLaughlin

Introduction

Pastoral care in schools has three elements: a welfare function, a control function and an educative function. These elements are seen in action in the curriculum, in work with groups, inside and outside the classroom, and in work with individuals. Much of the work on gender and schooling has focused on the curriculum, access to it, and on the school as an institution. In this chapter the emphasis will be on work with individuals. Watkins[1] has called this aspect of pastoral work, 'pastoral casework'.

'Pastoral casework' is that part of pastoral work which focuses on individuals and their personal and social development, on how they are progressing within the school setting and on their learning. Pastoral casework has a caring function, where the concern is the pupil's welfare; it may also have a control function, where the concerns may be disciplinary. There is also an educative function in work with individuals. Schools can plan provision for individuals, for example, through a framework for guidance, but there will be many unplanned dealings with individuals. In this chapter I shall look at the school's planned provision and also at the unplanned provision, ie the incidental work with individuals which focuses on their care and control. These are two very important arenas in which to examine gender. In the interactions between pupils, between teachers and pupils, and between teachers, the 'affective climate' of the school and the curriculum[2] is shaped and formed. Much of the interaction is to do with pupils' behaviour, standards and expectations, and can add to or detract from gender stereotypes. It will be influential in contributing to gender images.

Before moving on there is a need to note the danger of over-emphasising work with individuals. Sometimes dealing with an issue as the individual's problem can obscure the need to work at other levels eg class, group, year group or institutional. For example, an incident of aggressive behaviour which is being treated as the pupil's problem may also be an indication of issues which are school-or group-based. Watkins and Wagner[3] have warned us that the individual can be made a scapegoat in disciplinary matters. Williamson[4] has described a process he calls 'pastoralisation', where the pastoral care system of the school acts as a labelling agency, fulfilling the role of social controller. This process, he says, is unexamined. Work with individuals should not be a substitute for other activities which may be more appropriate, if pastoral casework is to be more than blind socialisation.

In our work with individuals we also need to remember the principle of empowerment. Central to the activities of guidance, counselling and gender work is the concept of empowering pupils to understand and act, rather than blindly obey. This point has many implications. First, it affects the way in which individual incidents are handled, since advising, supporting, guiding and disciplining should aim to help the pupil understand herself and share the grounds for action. It should be educative. Second, it means that individual guidance and support may not be enough. Pupils also need to have the opportunity to act. The classic, much – quoted example is that of decision-making. It is not enough to work with John on how to make a considered decision if John is never given the opportunity in school to make one. Pastoral casework is to do with supporting and guiding individual pupils but it needs to be set within the wider context of the school.

Planned work with individuals

The principle that schools should *plan* their provision for work with individuals, rather than letting it occur haphazardly, is an important one. During the planning process, provision is examined and can be made available to all pupils, rather than those who shout loudest and longest. The notion of 'compulsion' is one that has come to be seen as very important in work on sex differentiation. If 'work' with individual pupils is left to chance and demand, then we are, in fact, condoning the forces of differentiation which are at work. We are assuming a stance of gender blindness, for unplanned work can collude with differentiation.

Unplanned work may amount to gender blindness, since although effective guidance has a number of common principles, Watts and Kant[5] argue that differentiation between the sexes can be seen. They cite the following as examples of socialising influences which affect the choices of career which boys and girls might make:

- different socialisation so that girls have lower educational and occupational aspirations;

- the sexual differentiation in schooling which encourages different educational experiences for boys and girls, and thus different qualifications;
- pressures on girls to enter traditionally 'female' and often low-paid jobs, such as nursing;
- difficulties and retrictions as a result of child-rearing and domestic responsibilities.

There have not not been many studies of guidance systems in relation to gender, but some have suggested[6,7] – and I would agree – that 'counselling services provided for students generally support and reinforce stereotyped attitudes and behaviours about appropriate roles for males and females in society.'[8]

What is meant by planned work?

There are a range of activities and processes through which guidance may by offered to individuals. A useful framework is given by Miller in the FEU (1982) document of tutoring (see Figure 8.1).[9]

These different activities constitute parts of the process of guidance. Schools need to examine what is needed for individual pupils in the following areas.

Figure 8.1 A range of activities and processes through which guidance may be offered.

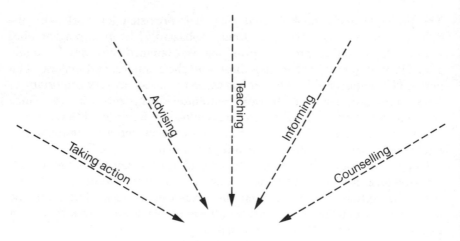

Enabling self-reliance

1 *Personal guidance*, which focuses on personal needs and is concerned with developing self-awareness.
2 *Educational guidance*, which focuses on learning, learning provision and individual needs.
3 *Vocational guidance*, which focuses on career choice/progression and access to employment
4 *Discipline and control*, which focuses on how rules, standards, and actions of pupils are dealt with.

Counselling and guidance – general issues

Before going on to look at these four categories of personal, educational, vocational and disciplinary guidance there is a need to examine some general issues which relate to gender. Before a teacher and pupil get together, actions will have been taken that affect what happens when they do get together. Decisions such as who and what sort of behaviour or circumstance call for an intervention, who will provide it, and what sort of intervention is provided, will all be affected by gender.

The circumstances of intervention – who and what

First, the perception of the need for a guidance or counselling intervention is related to schools' and teachers' awareness of gender issues. If a school or teacher does not perceive that there are gender issues in careers counselling or educational counselling, for example, then no planned intervention will take place; neither will it be monitored. It is by no means self-evident that everyone is aware of the gender issues. Yet, to take an example, there is evidence[10] that girls wanting to enter non-traditional forms of work report attempts by teachers to dissuade them. Girls and boys who choose to enter a non-traditional form of work may need support, but it will not be given unless the teachers see the need to intervene.

A girl and boy may perform the same action and it may be reacted to in a very different way. A girl's behaviour may be labelled 'agressive' because of stereotypes about girls as quiet and 'ladylike'. Similarly, I have heard discussions about 'effeminate' boys and their need to be counselled, which suggest that non-stereotyped behaviour can be seen as an appropriate reason for a referral for counselling. There is evidence that we react differently in schools to the same behaviour on the basis of gender. Shaw[11] has shown that girls absent from school are less likely to be labelled as 'truant' and more likely to be labelled 'non-attender'. The milder label may lead to a gentler action or to a different type of intervention from that given to a boy.

Who intervenes?

In many schools the person who delivers the guidance and counselling is matched by gender to the pupils who are identified as in need. Job descriptions for posts of deputy head or pastoral leader often contain prescriptions about work with one or other of the sexes. The phrase 'responsible for girls' discipline and welfare' still appears in many job descriptions for female teachers. Such actions reinforce the idea that only members of the same sex can control and understand each other. It is also inadvertently saying something about the type of response open to girls and boys or the range of responses which they will receive, but this will be looked at in the next section.

What sort of intervention?
John Heron[12] offered a classification of interventions. He suggests two main categories of intervention: facilitative and authoritative. He then sub-divides there into a number of categories, which are not hierarchically related. (see Figure 8.2) This is a useful guide to the range of interventions open to us and adds to the FEU (1982) framework previously mentioned. The reason for including it here, apart from its usefulness, is that there is a possibility that we may restrict the nature of our interventions on a gender basis. There is still the common belief that certain emotional responses are gender – related and this belief may dictate the nature of the intervention. Whyld states that,

> Girls may be better served than boys by counselling, since it is assumed that girls are more emotional and need to discuss their problems more. However, dwelling on the emotional is generally regarded as a sign of weak character, so unless there is an obvious problem, boys will be encouraged to 'keep their chin up'.[13]

Given the above, then a boy may be offered an authoritative intervention such as 'What do you plan to do about this?' rather than a facilitative one,

Figure 8.2 Types of Intervention

Facilitative

Cathartic	Aims to release feelings
Catalytic	Aims to help the other to rethink or re-examine
Supportive	Aims to support and affirm worth

Authoritative

Prescriptive	Aims to direct behaviour by instructing, advising or evaluating.
Informative	Aims to impart new knowledge.
Confronting	Aims to challenge or give direct feedback.

J. Heron

such as 'How do you feel about this now?' Girls, however, may not be offered authoritative interventions, such as 'You seem to just follow in groups and yet I see you as being a strong leader.' Heron does say that he feels professionals are generally more skilled in the authoritative interventions and less skilled in the facilitative ones.

These then are factors for teachers to reflect upon, for they are the foundation stones of the guidance framework. Decisions made at this fundamental level beforehand will affect what happens later, at another level, within the teacher – pupil sessions.

Some questions a tutor or teacher might ask about their practice, which relate to the points made, are:

1 Am I aware that there may be gender issues in counselling work?
2 Are different labels given to the same action performed by a boy or girl?
3 Are different responses given to boys and girls who behave in the same way?
4 Are pupils referred on the basis of gender stereotypes?

I would now like to move on to look at planned work with individuals under four main headings – personal, educational, vocational guidance and disciplinary interventions.

Personal guidance and counselling

The phrase 'intervention' was used earlier. The word is not intended to imply 'unsolicited interference'[12]. When using the term 'counselling' there is an assumption that work with pupils will be *invitational*. This is not to imply that all pupils have to self-refer or knock on the door with an articulately expressed need for counselling! It is to say that at some point the pupil will be offered a choice, eg 'Would you like to talk about this?'

There is a danger that in being well-meaning we can invade personal rights. There is a specific issue here about gender stereotypes and expectations. Sometimes our own expectations about what is gender-appropriate behaviour can lead us to perceive that a pupil has a 'problem' when, in fact, the problem is with our perception and inability to tolerate difference or ambiguity. This makes the offering of an 'invitation' important. It is not to imply that a teacher should never approach a pupil or initiate an intervention if the teacher feels that the pupil is experiencing a difficulty. Part of the school's guidance function is to observe and monitor pupils who may be experiencing some personal or other difficulty and offer the opportunity for counselling, be it inside or outside the school setting, and whatever the circumstances in which it is offered personal guidance and counselling work is almost inevitably going to touch on issues of gender image and expectations of gender role.

As adolescents are in a time of identity formation and are often seriously exploring relationships, gender image will be involved. Wall[14] shows that during adolescence the young person is concerned with learning about her or his bodily self, sexual self, social self, vocational self and philosophical self. Others[15] have added the self as learner and organisational self to this list. Personal counselling will focus on many of these selves. In this section I shall discuss the sexual, bodily and social self primarily, leaving the vocational and the self as learner until later. Obviously, not all counselling work is to do with gender but there is a need to be aware of the significance of what might be said and how our focus, or lack of it, may affect a pupil's development. I shall illustrate these points by referring to my own work with pupils. Mandy was referred to me for help, when I was working as a school counsellor, because she was experiencing difficulties in class. She was described as 'disruptive' and 'unco-operative' and was perceived as being 'at risk'. The focus for the referral was her inappropriate behaviour in class. She was also a cause for concern because of her sexual behaviour. She was seemingly more interested in her relationships with boys than with her school progress. This behaviour took the form of hanging around the boys' toilets and indulging in 'horseplay'.

During the course of our work it became clear that a major issue was her perception of her worth as a girl and in particular, her body image. Mandy came from a family of four children, three boys and herself. Her mother had fixed perceptions of what was appropriate behaviour for a girl and a boy. Part of this set of expectations was that 'female' matters were not to be discussed and were to be kept hidden from the males in the family. Mandy had just begun to menstruate and the messages she was getting were that this was to remain hidden from the males in the family as it was 'dirty'. These messages went deep into her perceptions of herself as a girl. She was beginning to develop very negative feelings about herself and they were related to her femaleness. This process was compounded by family expectations that she would do the domestic chores and that her brothers would not. She began to see being a female as a dirty and punishing thing. Her confusion about her gender worth lead her to experiment with it in other areas. She was attractive to boys and she experimented with this, often putting herself in situations of risk. Her feelings about her worth and the actions of her body could be said to be the focus of our work and her difficulties. What began as a school matter was intextricably linked to her gender image. If her early mention of her periods had not been taken seriously, then a negative body and gender image might have been reinforced with far-reaching consequences for her and her relationships.

Other writers have documented the area of body image and related it to incidents of sexual harrassment in schools. Bea Campbell[16] quotes from the words of 11 and 12-year-old girls in a south London comprehensive. 'It's as if the boys rule us and there's nothing you can do about it. They get girls in corridors and say "How big are your tits?" and start feeling them up. It makes you feel sort of terrible about your body'. In working with individuals there is a need to take seriously the full implications for a pupil's body and self-image of incidents such as these.

Sometimes how a pupil deals with issues of body image is perceived as gender inappropriate. Sue was referred to me for counselling because she was being 'aggressive'. She was small for her age and her schoolmates had nicknamed her 'midget'. Her reaction to this was to hit out and try to initimidate her taunters into submission. This was a response used by many of the boys in the school but there was concern that she, as a girl, was using this male coping strategy. I am not suggesting that her actions should have been condoned or that they were not problematic for her, but that the referral was based on a teacher's perception of gender – appropriate behaviour. Sue had problems with her body image and she was concerned also that her responses were seen as masculine. She was confused by the implications for her view of her sexual self.

The two examples I have given have been of girls: this is not to imply that the area of sexual and body image are only issues for girls. Similar preconceptions and issues arise for boys.

Sex education and guidance
Recently, the area of sex education and guidance on sexual matters has become controversial. There is a need in this highly emotional climate to return to the evidence. Various studies have been done on the amount of sex education that young people receive and on the quality and source of it. In the mid-1970s Farrell[17] found that teenagers got the bulk of their information from their friends. Balding's study[18] found that this was still the case for 39% of boys and 33% of girls. Parents were the primary source for girls and the second source for boys. Allen's study[19] found that parents and teenagers considered school to be the most important source and said that school should provide sex education and guidance. Schools were seen as highly credible. In the same study Allen found that 58% of boys and 31% of girls had never spoken to their mothers on any of the 14 sex – related topics, and the majority, 72%, had never spoken to their fathers. These results underline the importance of sex education and guidance in schools and have obvious implications for a school's planned provision, but they also highlight the need for boys to receive extra help. There is renewed evidence that boys still tend to miss out on sex education both at home and at school (see also National Children's Bureau Highlight No 81[20]).

Allen's evidence is that sex education from both home and school is effective in enhancing responsible behaviour.

> Openness about sex may be an especially important factor in lowering adolescent fertility...and...teenage pregnancy rates are lower in countries where there is a greater availability of contraceptive services and of sex education.[21]

I have felt the need to rehearse the need for and efficacy of sex education and guidance in schools as teachers are a little uncertain at the moment about the whole area.

The recent legislation which bears on the area of individual guidance is the Education (No 2) Act 1986 and section 28 of the Local Government Act 1988. The wider area of the Education Act (No 2) 1986 and sex education will not be discussed here: the focus will be on the area of individual guidance and counselling.

The Education Act (No 2) and the DES guidelines *Sex Education at School*[22] are not free from contradictions or tensions. The Act requires that schools, working through governing bodies, formulate a school policy on sex education. Teachers must be aware of the school's policy statement, for it is central here and must be followed. The DES circular does not prescribe the giving of advice, information or counselling. It states

> Good teachers have always taken a pastoral interest in the welfare and well-being of their pupils. But this function should never trespass on the proper exercise of parental rights and responsibilities.

One tension becomes apparent here. The previous evidence quoted shows that parents and pupils see the school as playing a very important role; sometimes parents in a sense give their rights to the school. Many young people feel that they cannot discuss sexual matters with their parents. The circular does acknowledge that teachers will find themselves in situations where the pupil may not want to tell their parents and the teachers may have to put the care and needs of the pupils first. This is not a new issue for teachers. This moral and professional dilemma has long been present. The DES acknowledge this. It states that where such a question arises, the action taken will 'depend on the particular circumstances involved and the professional judgement of the staff.'

Section 28 of the Local Government Act (1988) and the Education Act (1986) both deal with the issue of homosexuality and schools. The former forbids LEAs to 'promote homosexuality' and the DES circular on the implementation of the Education Act states that 'There is no place in any school in any circumstances for teaching which advocates homosexual experimentation by pupils.' (Section 22). This does not preclude the counselling of pupils about their feelings of homosexuality. The NUT recently said, 'There is a great deal of difference between providing information and promoting it.'[23] Teachers should continue to act in a humane fashion to pupils experiencing difficulties. Allen's study[19] shows that the subject least likely to arise out of the 14 topics listed is homosexuality, with only 4% of children having any information about it. The dangers here are of self-censorship and a climate which makes the discussion even more inclement and difficult.

150

This section has focused on guidance work in the areas of the bodily, sexual and social self. Some of this work has become contentious, but the evidence is that the teacher's role in helping young people is of paramount importance. Sound, professional work will not be threatened by recent legislation.

Some ways in which tutors and teachers can apply these points are summarised below.

1 Be aware of offering counselling to a pupil rather than forcing it on a pupil.
2 Listen out for statements from pupils which relate to body image and be aware of the need to take them seriously.
3 Take seriously incidents where boys or girls report sexual harrassment.
4 Monitor the sex education and guidance given to pupils, with a view to seeing that adequate provision is given to both sexes.

Educational guidance and counselling

In our work with pupils about their learning and progress one of the important areas is that of feedback and attribution. Various studies have shown that girls and boys tend to respond differently to reactions from adults about their performance. Boys tend to attribute lack of success to lack of effort, whereas girls attribute it to lack of ability. Carol Dweck has undertaken major research studies on this[24,25] and the main findings are summarised here

> Findings from numerous investigators of achievement behaviour provide evidence for the greater tendency of girls to attribute failure to uncontrollable factors like lack of ability...and to show disrupted performance and decreased achievement strivings under failure and evaluative pressure...and to avoid situations in which failure is likely... In contrast, boys in comparable evaluative situations tend to attribute their failure to controllable or variable factors, to show improvements in performance or increased achievement strivings, and to approach tasks that present challenges.[24]

The implications of new initiatives in assessment and testing need to be considered here in relation to the statement about 'evaluative situations'. In educational guidance work teachers need to help pupils to interpret, understand and use the feedback they receive.

'The pastoral task is to re-teach, or,...to give "attribution retraining".'[6] Teachers working in the area of pupil profiling and formative assessment will need to take account of Dweck's findings, especially in relation to the one-to-one dialogues about progress and future work, which form such a large part of so many schemes. Here is an arena for the re-teaching. As the number of formalised evaluations is likely to increase, teachers will need to help girls become aware of how they view assessments. If failure is not to be seen as uncontrollable, then girls will need assistance in placing the locus of control within, rather than outside, themselves ie so that a girl can say, 'I failed at this task, so how can I improve' rather than 'I am a failure. I can't do this subject.'

Dweck's findings also have implications for teachers and their own use of feedback. Teachers have been through a similar process during their own schooling, so the gender of the counsellor or guidance worker may well dictate how she or he copes with feedback on work undertaken with pupils. Teacher appraisal schemes could usefully note these findings.

Pupils' expectations of success are gender-related in another way, connected to gender perceptions of certain subject areas. There is now a wealth of evidence on the perceptions of subjects and their relationship to gender role.[26,13] If a boy is taking what is generally seen in his school as a 'female' subject then he is going to need support and special help, and this applies for girls in areas such as maths. Clearly there are implications for the curriculum and teaching methods, but also for the school and its planned guidance support. Sarah was a good example. As a form teacher, I worked with Sarah on her option choices during her third year and we talked about her career choice. She wanted to be an engineer. She chose technical drawing and was the only girl in a group of boys. I supported her at the time of her decision but planned no further. By the end of the fourth year Sarah had abandoned her desire to be an engineer saying, 'it was silly'. She really may have made a different choice but she was also not given the individual support needed to follow through her original, difficult plan of action.

Under the proposals for the National Curriculum it is likely that option choices will be reduced, but there may still be choices to be made about areas of study. The factors which influence subject choice are complex, but gender roles are likely to play an important part in influencing choice. For example, Grafton et al[27] showed that where subjects were theoretically open to both sexes, tutors influenced the decision by requesting boys to have prior discussions with the tutor where they wanted to opt for the family and child course. These problems require the school to act on a wider front than that of just individual guidance and conuselling. Where choices may affect vocational choice, careers counselling needs to take place as early on in the process as possible. Luxton[2] found in looking at schools' work on TVEI and gender that compulsion was central to access to the curriculum. When there was choice boys and girls made stereotypical choices: when there was compulsion boys and girls progressed well.

Vocational guidance and counselling

The vocational development of boys and girls has been receiving much attention recently under the Technical and Vocational Education Initiative, yet there is still evidence that the situation is not a balanced one in terms of gender. Hopkins[28] in a study of one LEA's TVEI programme, states 'traditional sex role stereo-typing still exists within TVEI... Not only is there evident sex role stereo-typing but despite high levels of measured ability amongst the girls, their teachers' perceptions of their ability is low, their own perception of their ability is low and their expectations are also low.' He goes on to say that 'although this brief paper discusses gender differentiation in only one TVEI authority, I am fairly certain that the picture is common to many other LEAs'. I have quoted Hopkins at some length in order to show the complexity and difficulty of the task, for the TVEI had lack of gender differentiation as an explicit aim and is still struggling to achieve it.

If schools are to work towards lack of gender differentiation in vocational choice, I would want to argue that sustained, planned individual guidance should be part of the strategy since we are dealing here with questions of an individual's identity. The sexual, bodily, social, philosophic, and self as learner are bound up in the vocational self. The development of the vocational self is 'essentially (a process) of developing and implementing a self-concept: it is a compromise process in which the self-concept is a product of inherited aptitudes, neural and endocrine make-up, opportunity to play various roles, and evaluations of the extent to which the results of role playing meet with the approval of superiors and fellows.'[29]

Vocational choice is inseparable from images of femininity, masculinity, perceptions of lifestyle and, for many girls, decisions about marriage and/or parenthood. As Hopkins stated, it is also linked to perceptions of ability, achievement and expectations of success and potential.

Law and Watts[30] offer a framework for vocational guidance. They see it as important that young people are helped to develop skills, attitudes and knowledge related to:

- *Opportunity awareness* – awareness of the range of possibilities that exist, the demands they make, and the rewards and satisfactions they can offer;
- *Self-awareness* – awareness of the distinctive characteristics that define the kind of person one is, and the kind of person one wishes to become;
- *Decision learning* – awareness of the styles in which decisions can be made, and acquisition of the skill that will help one to make decisions in a manner more satisfactory to oneself;
- *Transition learning* – acquisition of the awareness and skills needed to

cope with the transitions consequent upon one's decisions and with the new situations one will meet.

The development of these awarenesses and skills starts early and is inseparable from gender. 'With appropriate guidance, what might have been a conditioning process can be transformed into a learning process.'[5] Guidance work will be in groups, in curricular and extra-curricular work, but it needs also to be individual if it is to deal with the very personal and individual nature of the process of vocational development. Watts and Kant (1986) give very useful examples of guidance strategies in groups and in the curriculum, but I would argue that there needs to be a programme of individual guidance alongside other activities in the careers programme, and that it needs to begin early on in the secondary school. Hamblin's[31] questioning of pupils showed that pupils begin to make decisions about their employment, ability and potential as early as their first year in secondary education.

Tutors and teachers can be aware of:

- the individual support pupils may need in their choices of career path;
- the subtle ways in which adults can convey gender stereotypes eg by asking a pupil if he or she has 'really thought about' a choice;
- whether pupils need to learn skills or have certain experiences as part of their support.

Discipline and gender

The pastoral work of a school can often consist largely of work to do with discipline and behaviour. Recently, much evidence has been reported which shows that there is gender differentiation at work here.[13,32,33] These studies show that in one-to-one dealings with pupils, teachers discriminate and react differently on the basis of gender. Similar behaviours are treated differently, punishments and referrals may be affected, and incidents may or may not be followed up depending on the sex of the pupil.

One of the key issues here may be that of visibility or publicity. It would appear that boys are more active or visible in their deviance and girls more passive: similarly, there is some evidence that teachers respond in a less 'public' way to girls' deviance. To return to the point about involvement in deviance, Davies,[34] using a self-report schedule, found similar deviance levels for girls and boys. Lawrence, Steed and Young[35] studied an outer London comprehensive, and found boys were more involved in incidents than girls, by a ratio of 3:2. Watkins and Wagner[3] offer various interpretations. First, that girls' deviance is better hidden than boys'; second, that girls indulge in less challenging forms of deviance and are therefore less noticed; and third, that girls and teachers respond in a different way from boys and teachers when deviance is challenged. 'With the little reseach evidence available the last two explanations receive some support'.

Lawrence, Steed and Young[35] gave teachers a questionnaire which examined teacher responses to pupil behaviours. Teacher responses showed great differences when applied to girls and boys. Boys' behaviour called forth more 'emotional' responses than girls but female secondary teachers were more concerned about deviancy in girls. Signs of miserableness and unhappiness were spotted less often in boys by female teachers. The reasons for this may be to do with ability to empathise and that the traditional masculine 'stiff upper lip' role is hard to break through.

Further differences found in this study were to do with responses to deviant behaviour. Secondary teachers suggested more often that a girl should be referred to a doctor or child guidance clinic. This may be as a result of a cultural view of deviance as masculine and of deviance in girls as highly 'abnormal'. It may be that when a girl does indulge in very visible misbehaviour, it evokes an anxious response. Watkins and Wagner[3] state that 'problem' girls are seen as a 'bigger problem' than boys on occasion, when the deviance is of a challenging variety. And on other occasions a passive or evasive response may be tolerated more from a girl than it would from a boy.'

There are complex processes at work in teacher/pupil interactions to do with control. The DES[33] found that schools had different rules for behaviour, dress and manners for boys and girls and as has been discussed, the way 'rules' are broken varies, as does teacher response. I have argued that an element of this process is visibility of behaviour. In the disciplining of pupils all these processes need to be examined if the aim is gender equity.

Unplanned work with individuals

This section aims to look at the unplanned interactions between pupils and pupils, teachers and teachers, and pupils and teachers. There is considerable overlap with the previous section for each of the areas described in section one will have significance in incidental provision, but, there are differences.

It is in the school's incidental work, in the area of the 'hidden curriculum' that powerful messages are sent. It is in this sphere that intentions and the state of teachers' awareness of their learnings about gender can be clearly seen. Teachers hold widely different positions about gender dependent upon age, subject specialism, sex, personal experience and even regional location. Teachers' learning will be displayed in their one-to-one interactions with other staff and with pupils. These interactions are very powerful in shaping the affective climate of the school and can even have the power to undermine planned provision if they are in opposition to it. Pupils will learn from teachers about expectations, appropriate behaviour, role, and acceptable values from behaviour between staff and towards pupils.

Gender can be an issue in the affective climate or ethos of a school and can deeply affect the welfare and learnings that take place in a school setting. If stereotypical behaviours are expected of men, women, boys and girls, then teachers and pupils will be restricted in terms of their gender development. If one set of stereotypes values predominate ie 'male' or 'female' ones, then there is even more limitation.

There is a need to handle these matters with sensitivity and with an awareness of the social and cultural climate of the school, for these are attitudes and behaviours which have been learned slowly and, to a large extent, unconsciously. To challenge the attitudes of teachers or pupils head on and in an unsystematic, unsympathetic fashion will be to harden, strengthen, and potentially exacerbate the problem. Teachers can use their knowledge about learning to good effect here. Teachers are acting out their own learnings about gender and the affective element of this needs to be acknowledged and understood for constructive change to take place.

In what areas of their incidental work with individuals might teachers display these learnings and how might pupils learn from them? One area is work which has a guidance focus, ie the reprimanding, praising, encouraging and modifying of pupil behaviour. The question is whether there is gender differentiation here. Gender can be an unhelpful focus eg The boy who is called a 'girl' or 'woman' as a form of control and derogation is receiving messages about the worth of girls and boys, as well as having limits put on his acceptable responses. Another area is teachers' naming and labelling of actions for these will have great significance to pupils. Dweck's[24,25] previously mentioned work on feedback is also very relevant here. How I explain or react to the failure or success of an action can affect the interpretation a pupil makes of the reasons for her or his success or failure. Similarly significant is my interpretation to other teachers of pupil's success or failure.

Here I have focused on teacher/pupil interaction but teacher/teacher interaction is important too. Teachers can and do label each other, sometimes with an unhelpful gender link, for example, teachers can sometimes be divided by a false polarity between 'hard' and 'soft' in terms of styles of keeping order. Where this is linked to gender it is destructive. Teachers too can experience difficulty concerning gender issues in schools. Since teachers' behaviours and attitudes about gender are learned and the school is a sexed environment, then this is not surprising. Whyld[13] gives an example of a possible dilemma for a female teacher. 'If she admits that she is intimidated by male pupils, she will not be seen as an able teacher, will jeopardize chances of promotion and other jobs, and may feel she is showing up all women as having special problems because of their sex.' As well as anxieties about classroom interactions and gender, teachers may have anxieties about one-to-one, more private interactions. A male teacher recently discussed with me his worries about being alone in a room with a female pupil during interviews for records of achievement. His learnings about gender were at work. He felt he should fear this situation for it may be dangerous.

This section has examined the incidental work with individual pupils and how these individual unplanned interactions, alongside teacher-to-teacher communication, can combine to create a powerful affective climate. This ethos is the context for planned provision and can dramatically alter and affect the intended work on gender. Both these areas combine to shape what pupils learn about their worth and role in relation to their gender. Schools make a difference and they can examine what pupils are learning or they can pass on, partly through work with individuals, the unexamined learnings of the past; at worst they can amplify sex differences.

References

1   Watkins, C. (1985) 'Does pastoral care = PSE?' in *Pastoral Care in Education*. Vol 3. No 3. pp 179–183.
2   Luxton, R. (1987) Unpublished lecture. Hertford Teacher's Centre.
3   Watkins, C. and Wagner, P. (1987) *School Discipline*. Blackwell.
4   Williamson, D. (1980) 'Pastoral Care or Pastoralization?' in Best, R. et al (1980) (eds) *Perspectives on Pastoral Care*. Heinemann.
5   Watts, A. and Kant, L. (1986) *A Working Start: Guidance Strategies for Girls and Young Women*. Longman for School Curriculum Development Committee.
6   Marland, M. (ed.) (1983) *Sex Differentiation and Schooling*. Heinemann.
7   Wittig, M. and Petersen, A. (1979) *Sex-Related Differences in Cognitive Functioning*. Academic Press.
8   Saario, T. T. (1976) 'Title IX: Now what?' in Ornskein, A. and Miller, S. *Policy Issues in Education*. Levington Barker, DC Health.
9   Miller, J. (1982) *Tutoring*. FEU/Longman.
10 Benett, Y. and Carter, D. (1982) *Sidetracked? A look at the careers advice given to fifth form girls*. Equal Opportunities Commission.
11 Shaw, J. (1983) Open University Course. E353. Block 5. Open University Press, Milton Keynes.
12 Heron, J. (1975) *Six Category Intervention Analysis*. University of Surrey.
13 Whyld, J. (1983) *Sexism in the Secondary Curriculum*. Harper and Row, London.
14 Wall, W. D. (1974) *Constructive Education for Adolescents*. UNESCO/Harrap.
15 Hamblin, D. H. (1978) *The Teacher and Pastoral Care*. Blackwell.

16 Campbell, Bea in Whyld, J. (1983) *Sexism in the Secondary Curriculum.* Harper and Row.

17 Farrell, C. (1976) *My mother said...Study of the way young people learned about sex and birth control.* Routledge and Kegan Paul.

18 Balding, J. (1975) *Exploring Sex Messages with the Health-Related Questionnaire.* Values 2.1.

19 Allen, I. (1987) *Education in Sex and Personal Relationships.* Policy Studies Institute.

20 National Children's Bureau (1988) *Sex Education – a review of research.* Highlight no 81.

21 Jones, E. et al (1985) 'Teenage Pregnancy in Developed Countries'. Family Planning Perspectives 17, 2.

22 DES (1987) *Sex Education at School.* Circular 11/87. HMSO.

23 The Teacher 6.9.88 'Chaos reigns as clause 28 becomes law.'

24 Dweck, C. and Licht, D. (1983) 'Sex differences in learned helplessness.' *Developmental Psychology.* 12, pp 147–56.

25 Dweck, C. and Licht, D. (1983) 'Sex differences in achievement orientation' in Marland, M. (ed.) *Sex Differentiation and Schooling.* Heinemann.

26 Open University Course E205 *Gender Differentiation in Schools.* Open University Press, Milton Keynes.

27 Grafton et al (1983) 'Gender and curriculum choice' in Hammersley, M. and Hargreaves, A. (eds.) *Curriculum practice: some sociological perspectives.* Falmer Press.

28 Hopkins, D. (1986) TVEI Working Papers. 2. CARE, University of East Anglia.

29 Super, D. (1980) 'Approaches to Occupational Choice and Career Development' in Watts, A. et al (1981) *Career Development in Britain.* CRAC Hobsons Press.

30 Law, B. and Watts, A. G. (1977) *Schools, Careers and Community.* Church Information Office.

31 Hamblin, D. H. (1986) *A Pastoral Programme.* Blackwell.

32 Lawrence, J. et al (1984) *Disruptive Children? Disruptive Schools?* Croom Helm.

33 DES (1975) *Educational Survey 21.* HMSO

34 Davies, L. (1979) 'Deadlier than the male? Girls' conformity and deviance in school' in Barton, L. and Meighan, R. (eds) *Schools, Pupils and Deviance.* Nafferton Books.

35 Lawrence, J., Steed, D. and Young, P. (1981) *Dialogue on Disruptive Behaviour.* PJD Press.

9

Developing a gender sensitive practice in working with families

Patsy Wagner

This chapter aims to explore the issues which the pastoral team need to address in developing a gender-sensitive practice for work with pupils' families. This should become part of the school's policy on equal opportunities, entitlement and access.

In this chapter the word family is used to denote a grouping of people including at least one child, in which one or more of the adults has parental responsibility for the child/children. It could, of course, also be used to refer to groups of people without children. The word 'household' is used to refer to the people who live in the home of the pupil.

The chapter has two parts:

1 The first part deals with ideas and information about what constitutes a family, about the trends in patterns of relationships and arrangements for childrearing in families; this leads into a consideration of some of the gender issues which occur in families and their effects.
2 The second part deals with communicating with parents; it begins with a rationale for working with parents and families and goes on to consider ways of developing a range of activities in the home-school programme, the issues to be addressed and the skills which are needed.

Within the two parts, the sections in **bold type** denote activities which could be extracted for use in training sessions. These have been designed so that they could be used by the individual reader as well as by teams or groups of teachers as part of their professional development/as part of Inset sessions in schools.

Families and family patterns

We all have ideas and beliefs about what a family is, and about how various members behave within families according to their position and role (based on their age, sex, generation – child, parent, grandparent etc and kinship). For example, we all have some ideas about what we think might constitute a 'typical' family unit; we all have some ideas about what the 'typical' role(s) of a mother might be. These ideas vary from person to person depending on the experiences they have had, the examples they have come across, and the explorations they have made into their assumptions and into the issues. So, if we were to take a cross-section of the population and ask them about what they thought constitutes a family, about how the roles of different family members vary, or how different family members typically relate to each other, there would be enormous variations in the views that are held. We would also find that, whereas some people have less fixed views, others often hold their views as if they represent norms in society. We are all to some extent susceptible to this tendency to represent our own experience as 'absolute'. This is unsurprising, since people tend to form their views about families through their own family experience which is powerful and affecting.

In summary, a person's understanding of families is influenced primarily by the family in which s/he was brought up, as well as by the context and the structure of the culture and the society in which that family live which interacts with the familial influences. Social structure and cultural context are both, undoubtedly, powerful in the construction of an individual's ideas, expectations, belief systems and in the roles s/he adopts. In this analysis, however, the emphasis is mainly on making sense of the family and its influence on the individual.

For most people the family is a person's initial reference point and guide, and with age and experience a person affiliates more or less to the values and beliefs of the family. Each individual, however, has a unique experience in a family; we might expect, therefore, that life within a family would help its individual members understand more about diversity. But this does not generally seem to be the case. Rather, it seems that being a member of a particular family tends to engender a particular (family) view on particular issues and on how family members think and relate. This does not in any way mean that all family members will agree on these issues or will feel happy about these ways of relating. But each individual in a particular family will understand and find it difficult to resist being organised (in some way or other) by family views, through a process of either identifying with them, or opposing them. An outsider to that family might not even recognise the issue or difficulty when it arose in the family discourse or inter-relationships. To illustrate this point – many very competent adults find that, on occasions when they visit their family of origin, they suddenly find themselves reacting and responding to other family members in ways that surprise them. The experience is as if they are catapulted back in time. Suddenly old patterns of interaction (sometimes pleasurable but often uncomfortable or even painful), which they thought they had left behind in childhood or adolescence, re-emerge. This would not happen to this person in a different social context, but in their own family context the pattern of actions and reactions is relatively easily triggered by a particular situation. Families are, therefore, powerful social contexts which affect a person's beliefs and behaviours and the assumptions that people make about the beliefs and behaviours of others.

The implications of all of this are that, when we come to work with families, we need to take time to examine our own personal assumptions about families and roles in families (in addition to the assumptions of the society in which we live and of the institutions in which we work). We need also to acknowledge changing family patterns and different family experiences and realities so that we avoid conveying to pupils or their families assumptions based on our own particular experiences, generalisations or stereotypes. All of this is fundamental to establishing a gender-sensitive practice.

Changing family patterns

'The family is simply what you find behind the door' (Pugh & D'Eath 1984).

The arrangements people make for rearing their children are many and varied. The 'norm' of the two-parent family with mother at home and father at work and two children under 16, found in so many works of children's fiction, occurs in only 5% of families. The trends are clearly towards more diversity in family arrangements. Many people now delay marrying or choose not to marry. Once married, many people divorce: the current divorce figures indicate that one in three marriages now ends in divorce. Many people also then re-marry, and remarriages are even more likely than first marriages to end in separation. The number of step-parent families has also increased. Frequently, re-married couples go on to have children together in addition to the children of their previous marriages – so the number of children with step-parents and step-brothers or sisters has also increased. There are also now more single parent households – one in seven of all families. 80% of these single parents will have experienced the death, separation or divorce of a partner. A few will be teenage parents. The majority of the rest will be women who have chosen to be single parents and to raise children in households in which they are the sole parent. Often this will have been as a positive choice. A few single parents will be men. Some families will comprise homosexual couples. All of these family arrangements need to be anticipated by schools and efforts made to be aware of the facts and to understand and address the issues, rather than to make assumptions and/or value judgements.

Schools need to acknowledge that **divorce is now more common** than it was in previous generations and that this fact of life requires understanding and tact. The reasons for divorce are generally to do with some form of relationship breakdown. There will be different precipitating factors in different cases, and different effects. The most frequent causes for the breakdown of marriage seem to relate to the age and stage of the couple at the time of the marriage, the reasons that led to the marriage, and cultural expectations about marriage and divorce. For example, some couples will have married as a way of escaping from their family of origin, and the younger the couple are at the time the more likely there is to be a breakdown later (especially if the young person was unhappy in the family of origin). Pressure from within the family can be a factor which precipitates an early marriage, and social pressure can result in an ill-considered marriage. Some of these marriages will be successful, depending on how these factors and pressures cluster in particular cases, and on the social and cultural expectations and constraints experienced by the couple. Sometimes the breakdown will be concealed within the family because of cultural or familial expectations. Other marriages may quietly disintegrate. Some couples outgrow each other and part in later life when their paths become too divergent. For many it is the unexpected strain of child-rearing which puts the relationship between the couple under excessive strain. For others unemployment produces unbearable family stress and precipitates breakdown and separation or divorce. In some marriages patterns of violence and abuse lead to breakdown. These patterns may also occur in unmarried couples, resulting in separations.

Single handed parenting is frequently the arrangement made in a family for parenting. In some families a parent will be raising a child single handed because of a relationship breakdown. Most commonly this will be a woman. In other families the situation may be entirely different since there has been a conscious decision by one person to rear children as a single parent from the outset. Others do so because one partner is absent (for reasons which make sense for the family), in others because the parent is in a transition between relationships. Some will ostensibly be single parents but will constitute a family with a partner who does not form part of the household. Similarly, relations, friends, a network of friends, an extended family, or a variation on all of these can constitute a significant family group.

In all of these cases of single parents, schools often make erroneous judgements about the negative effects of single handed parenting – especially so if the child is raised by a man as a single parent. These judgements are undermining to the women and men who raise their children as single

162

parents and also to their children. They are often highlighted by errors about who is the 'head' of the household, and by the erroneous use of titles, such as Mrs when Miss or Ms. is more accurate (although single or unmarried women often use the title Mrs in anticipation of the school's embarrassment). So schools need to clarify the picture with sensitivity. One way to do this is to enquire tactfully, at the interview on entry to the school, about the name of the child as possibly distinct from the name(s) of the parent(s)/guardian(s). Similarly, the title(s) preferred by adult careers should be established and not assumed, and all of this information should be regularly updated.

The practice of **shared responsibility for child rearing** both in and out of a licensed marriage is prevalent. Some of these adults are couples, and these couples are varied; eg heterosexual married couples, unmarried heterosexual couples, homosexual (lesbian or gay) couples. Families in which one of the couple is a step-parent are very common, including those in which there are children from two different sets of parents and a child of the current pairing. All of these possibilities should be expected.

Other arrangements for childcare involved **a range of significant adults**. In some families a parent shares the child rearing with female relatives or friends, in others with men and women relatives or friends, or extended family members, neighbours, or child-minders. All of these people can form an important part of the family network for child care. Each of these arrangements is, potentially, equally valid, yet it seems that schools often convey the impression that all children come from families with married parents, both with the same surname as each other and their children, with mother at home looking after the children and father at work. This is rather surprising since there are just as many single parents, step-families, homosexual and lesbian couples etc in teachers' families as in the rest of the population. The main point in all of this is that schools need to make more explicit an acceptance, welcome, understanding and flexibility toward all of these families. This means examining policies, procedures and practices for underlying stereotypical assumptions – and then changing them!

Relationship breakdowns raise other issues for the school. There is now such a high rate of breakdown in adult relationships that we might reasonably expect schools to have considerable knowledge and expertise in supporting children through the experience. Schools can, indeed, be very helpful and supportive to families, for example, when there are negative effects on a child's progress in school. Parents may need support too, since children are often resistant to parents separating. In these cases children often fail to see and understand the couple's problems, especially when the child continues to have good relations with each parent. Parents often, inadvertently, collude with this by 'protecting' their children from the truth about their relationship.

The outcomes and effects of separations can, however, be very much more positive for both adults (and children) than a life together of continuing fights and recriminations, of withdrawal and despair, or boredom and frustration. But they may be events which children find incomprehensible and undermining of their confidence and self-esteem. Whatever the cause and the final outcome, the process of any relationship breakdown is bound to have effects on children. Schools need to convey a clear message of acceptance, so that adults are first of all prepared to say **when** they feel the child may be upset by events at home. Schools need to be sensitive to the possible effects on the child, for example, on a child's social and learning behaviour, or in her levels of attainment. It is important to let the parents know when these changes occur and involve them in trying to help the young person understand what is happening, and to develop coping strategies. This last point is most important: the pastoral team needs to be clear that sympathy and understanding of a pupil's difficulties is insufficient on its own. Informed and sensitive action is also required. **The school has a professional responsibility to try to help the pupil develop coping strategies to deal with any disruptive effects of separation and loss so that success in learning can continue.** Sometimes the parent will be in an extremely distressed state and teachers may feel that communication with home is too difficult – but neither upset nor anger nor any other communication difficulties should stand in the way of helping parents and families in the task of understanding and supporting their children so that those children are able to benefit from educational opportunities.

There are particular **issues for step-families** which schools need to be aware of. Families which comprise a step-parent (whether as a remarried heterosexual couple, or a partnership for living and child rearing) are a common family arrangement in which the couple will have worked out, in some way or other, how the responsibility for the children will be shared. In the case of such families being formed when the children are very young it can be easier for the couple to feel, and to work out, an equal responsibility for, and commitment to, the children. In the case of older children, the 'birth' parent can tend to feel and wish to exercise the major responsibility for the child, with the partner providing support for that in varying degrees. The school will be able to relate more appropriately to the family when these issues are clarified. How these are clarified is, of course, critical to good home-school relations. In many cases there may be a parent living in another household who retains an interest and a commitment to the child and the child's education. This other parent may not be the main caregiver, but in law will often have equal rights in relation to the pupil's education. All of these issues need to be addressed in the school's home-school relations policy so that teachers and parents are helped to be as supportive as possible to the success of pupils in school.

In some situations involving **divorced or separated couples** the school may need to use a great deal of diplomacy and tact. Relationships between a divorced or separated couple may be extremely strained and access arrangements may be fraught or in dispute. A child can sometimes be used by an adult who wishes to manipulate an ex-partner. In some cases children (and their mothers) may live in fear because of abusing ex-partners. In those cases when women or children have been physically and/or sexually abused by ex-partners (and maybe continue to be), or are being harassed following separation, the school will need to be understanding of the situation, vigilant over the mother and child's safety, clear about the local education authority's policy and procedures for engaging professional agencies, about the limits of the school's responsibilities, and the particular responsibilities of the statutory agencies in cases of abuse.

When couples are in conflict it can be difficult for the caring adults to be as helpful as they might ideally wish to be to their children over maintaining relationships with an ex-partner. Schools can be most helpful by listening carefully, by supporting the rights of the child, and by working to maintain positive relationships with both parents (when this is appropriate). What schools need to be clear about in these cases is that the child has a basic right to a relationship with both parents should s/he wish for it, and also a right to decline a relationship. Here, again, it will be important that there is a school policy which is communicated to all teachers on these issues, and that there is training for staff in understanding the issues and handling situations which may arise.

Bereavement raises a different but related set of issues. All families experience death at some time or other. Sometimes this is the death of an aged relative and as such is a sad loss which can have elements of relief at the release from, or avoidance of, an illness. In some families death comes unexpectedly through violence, or following an illness. The death of a partner, a child or sibling is a highly traumatic event in any family. When a separation comes as a result of death the response of the school will depend on how prepared the school staff and the pupils are for such events. In a society in which there is a tendency to sweep death under the carpet, it is no surprise that neither schools, teachers nor pupils feel prepared when a pupil is bereaved. There seems to be little systematic planning for such events and an inappropriate expectation that everything will be back to 'normal' in a very short length of time. An adult will normally take a minimum of a couple of years, and often much longer, to go through the mourning process following a significant bereavement. There is little to suggest that children are any different in these matters. Yet there is an incomplete understanding shown by schools of the process of mourning and the long-term effects of bereavement, divorce, illness or separation on families and children. Schools need to think seriously about including a consideration of loss and mourning in their personal-social curriculum so that there is better understanding of, and preparation for, those occasions when death occurs. There should also be agreed procedures and practices in the school to help children cope with the effects of death in the family. Children and young people need at these times to be supported appropriately and helped to keep some continuity and regularity in their lives at school. They can be helped to continue making progress in school by developing effective strategies to deal with the preoccupation and loss of concentration which normally accompanies a loss of this sort. This can only be done by the school prioritising the issues in their In-service training and in their curriculum development plans.

It is clear from all of this that the family arrangements and patterns of relationships which make up the experience of family life are many and varied. If we wish to work effectively with the whole range of families represented by the pupils we teach we should not, therefore, make any assumptions or value judgments about families based on simple stereotypes. We should, instead, ensure that we have sensitive ways of establishing who are the principle care-givers, and of communicating with them appropriately and engaging them effectively over that part of the education of their children which takes place in school. The practical details of all of this will be examined in the second section of this chapter. But first, in order to get a fuller picture of the issues that need to be addressed in developing effective and sensitive home-school relationships, it will be necessary to look at gender issues in families and at the effects of gender roles on girls and boys, and women and men.

Practical applications

> **Information and ideas from the above section could be used in training sessions: to raise awareness and sensitivity to the issues; to examine views of families and family patterns; to discuss and to develop appropriate responses in school.**

> **Discussion of the effects of separation and loss would constitute a useful session/series of sessions on working with pupils and parents; examination of the possible issues for bereaved parents of either sex, based on possible stereotyping over gender issues related to child care; practical approaches to talking with bereaved children and parents could be the focus of a series of sessions;**

> **Personal experience of course participants can be a useful way of exploring the variety of family arrangements and experiences of loss and the range of responses which are helpful and supportive. But note that, as in all sessions when personal experiences are elicited, all participants must be offered the option of contributing in other ways, and participants should not feel pressured to disclose personal information.**

Useful sources of input and support to the pastoral team in addressing these issues would be the educational psychology service; the child and family guidance services; the RE advisory service.

Gender issues and power in families

When we start to think about how to relate effectively to families, and how to help all pupils achieve in school, we need to have some understanding of gender issues in families and their effects. The writer of this chapter takes the position that:

The stereotyping of people on the basis of their sex deprives both women and men of opportunities which would allow them more options and choices in their lives about how they will be. Sexism, therefore decreases the potential of both women and men for fulfilment as multi-dimensional human beings.

In the family and in society **both men and women hold and wield particular forms of power.** This is a power over decision making. The areas of power tend to be separated out along the lines of sex, so that one sex seems to predominate in particular areas of power over the other, with the corollary that one or other of the sexes always seems to gain at the expense of the other (to the detriment of both men and women).

In the most general terms, it seems that men hold the most powerful and important positions in the society in which we live. That is to say, men are the main executors of economic power, which (however much we might disagree with it in principle), in a consumerist society, is considered the most important form of power. (The only really active example we have heard of to the contrary is of the women of Meghalaya in North West India who have a completely matriarchal society.)

Power in families relates to decision-making power in economic, emotional and social terms. Patterns in families seem, up to a point, to mirror the patterns in society. For example, one set of decisions in families, as in society, is about economic power, ie who decides how money is either earned, saved or spent. In many families and in many cultures the major decisions are ostensibly made by a man in the family who is considered the 'head' of the household and the 'breadwinner', in spite of the fact that many women work outside the family and contribute significantly to the family finances. The economic power that men wield within the family varies from family to family – there are regional differences, class differences, differences which relate to the ethnicity and culture of a particular family, and differences which relate to patterns of employment. But, in general, it still seems to be the case that men have more say in making what are considered the major financial decisions. Women, on the other hand, generally have more say over the day-to-day management of money – those aspects of household management which keep the family going, such as the purchase and preparation of food, which are often taken for granted and not credited as being important. Ironically, for many women their increased earning power outside the family has not been matched by an increase in their decision-making power within the family.

While men exercise more power in the economic domain, women, typically, exercise more power in the emotional and social domain of the family. The socialisation of men as the 'breadwinner' and 'head of the household' has led to the tendency for them to be more distant from the emotional domain of the family. Rather than the family, many men have tended to affiliate more to the social and emotional domain of the work place – whether this is the pub, the club, the office or the board room. The expectations that men's work is outside the family, and for that aspect of their lives to dominate, leads in most cases to them being less involved in the rearing of their children and hence less involved in the emotional life of the family. Institutions which relate to the family such as hospitals, schools and welfare services have colluded with this by approaching the women in families as the people responsible for the caring aspects of family life.

Families, schools and societies have particular expectations about the social and emotional development of boys and girls, and of the relative contribution of men and women in the rearing of children. Boys are usually reared and expected to be less expressive of their feelings, less responsive to the feelings of others and more direct and directive in their communication, whereas girls are usually reared to be more expressive of their feelings, more responsive to others, to express themselves more tentatively and to accomodate and be supportive to the communication of others. The experience of child rearing (predominantly carried out by women) develops the particular skills that girls are brought up to develop. It also tends to put women into contact with other women, so they also have more opportunity to develop and practise their social and relational skills in a childrearing context. Men, on the other hand, are more likely as adults to develop their social and relationship skills in the context of work. So their reason for relating to others has more possibility for being driven at some level by a form of economic necessity – to pull off a deal, to influence a client or colleague etc, rather than by the need to care for a child.

The skills and abilities that women and men have in the social and emotional domain are related to their sex. But this is to do with the gender roles they are prepared for rather than their biology and this preparation begins from an early age. In all families there will be some assumptions and expectations about gender roles based on the sex of a person. That is to say, in all families there are hidden rules about the the range of behaviours, tasks and responsibilities which are expected, tolerated, rewarded, approved or disapproved of, based on the sex (combined

168

with the age) of the person. Gender roles are determined to a large degree by the ethnicity, culture and class of the family. But each family has its own unique belief system derived from an admixture of the beliefs and behaviours, values and aspirations of previous generations, of significant social networks outside the family and of the norms of society. The way these have been received and acted upon by the individuals who make up the family, and the way those individuals have worked out some way of resolving any differences over those issues produces the complexity and the uniqueness of each family's belief system and of each individual's belief system within that family.

Schools need be aware that the variety of roles that women and men play in society and in families have been constructed and restricted by gender roles, and to ensure that they address the issues and avoid, as far as possible, mirroring and reinforcing unhelpful and negative stereotypes.

Practical applications

This activity can be carried out by the individual reader. It can also be used as an activity in a team meeting, workshop or INSET session in school, as a staff development exercise on gender roles and their effects.

Take the questions below and use them to explore the beliefs in your own family about gender roles. Consider to what extent your current beliefs and behaviours are organised (either through identity or opposition) in a range of situations by your family of origin;

1 How were girls and women/boys and men in my family and extended family expected to behave? What were the similarities and differences in expectations of the behaviour of boys and girls?

2 What particular roles and responsibilities were girls and boys and men and women expected to carry out in the family? How were they different?

3 What were the explicit and implicit messages and expectations about the differences between the sexes, over showing feelings and acting assertively, passively or aggressively?

4 What were the differences in the expectations and aspirations about family, jobs, careers?

Gender role stereotyping – the influences and effects

Gender role stereotyping is that process which attributes fixed traits to a person on the basis of their biological sex. It ignores individual preferences, interests and tendencies in favour of crude judgements about how men and women 'are' and what they want to be. It has damaging effects on women and men and boys and girls.

The influences which produce gender role stereotypes (and gender roles) operate at the levels of the family, the cultural and ethnic group to which that family belongs, the society in which they live and the institutions in which they work and in which their children are educated. These influences have a tendency to interact, exacerbate the problem and then compound the stereotype. The overall effect reduces the options available to women and men about how they will behave; it undermines and de-values women; it restricts the expressive capacities of men; and it damages the possibility for harmonious and fulfilling relationships between the sexes.

Families are a major influence on the development of gender roles. One aspect of the process occurs in the way that tasks and responsibilities are shared out. So, in most families in which there are children, women take a major responsibility for child rearing, for the caring and servicing of other adults and adult dependents, for managing the household, for managing the family's social network and its communications with the extended family. It seems that currently women are still mainly responsible for these aspects of family life, as well as going out to work. In other words it seems that in spite of the so-called liberation of women, they actually do more! Yet, at work women are still generally paid less than men (the average is 73% of what men earn), and in the home their work is taken for granted as unpaid, and considered part of their role as women. Some women find they can more or less cope with this state of affairs and still gain from rewarding relationships with their children and through the process of child rearing. Having said that, it comes as no real surprise to learn that more married, than unmarried, women suffer from psychiatric illness, whereas for men the converse is the case. So, it seems that, in general, marriage is hazardardous to the mental health of women and protective to that of men.

On the other hand the socialisation of men from an early age into their economic – 'breadwinning' – role and the power and position they hold in society because of this, comes at the expense of their emotional development, their physical health and, it seems, their longevity. At this point in

170

time men suffer more than women from what seem to be work-related and stress-induced illnesses, such as ulcers and heart attacks. And of those who work until 65, the majority die within three years of retirement. But there is also a worrying trend towards an increase in stress-related behaviours and health problems in women. Young adult women are now more likely than women of their mothers' generation to drink and smoke. This may reflect the stress resulting from the multiple roles, expectations and demands made on women in society. This is especially the case for women who combine work in and out of the home and childrearing. Children learn by the example of the adults around them and the expectations that are created in their families. In this way girls and boys are prepared by their families to perpetuate gender roles.

Sex roles in families can have a major influence on a pupil's level of aspiration and achievement in school. A girl in the nursery school will tend to play with toys that are familiar and in ways that seem familiar unless she is encouraged otherwise. For example, she may choose only to play with 'girl's' toys or games at school if these seem more familiar than the large construction toys. A boy in the nursery, on the other hand, may choose large construction toys and avoid activities requiring the use of fine motor skills in sticking, cutting or drawing. Aspirations are not always to do with success; a boy who is beginning reading may decide *not* to become a successful reader because of his father who is semi-literate. In the teenage years a young person is engaged in the task of working out for themselves the sort of person they want to be. In this search most young people start from the position of having some degree of identification with the values of their parents. Later on they may begin to question and oppose those values. But by that time they may have already made major choices and decisions about their interests and about the subjects they will follow in school. Sometimes a young person will want to choose a subject that does not fit with the family's view of what is appropriate for a boy or a girl and this will produce conflicts and divided loyalties. Schools will need to recognise all of these possible issues so that they can help pupils explore their talents and abilities and be successful in school. The school will also need to help parents and families to recognise and to celebrate all the talents that their children display without the constraints of gender stereotypes.

The success of pupils can only be fully achieved when schools start to work with parents to redress the negative effects of sex stereotyping. This leads us into the area of communication between school and home. The school has an important role in helping families understand the purposes of education, and in engaging the expertise and support of families in the process of schooling. The final part of this chapter, therefore, deals with working with families, with a focus on communication and gender issues.

This activity can be carried out by the individual reader, it can also be used as an activity in a team meeting, workshop or INSET session on: gender roles in families; the effects of gender stereotyping on pupils' aspirations in schools; the issues in addressing gender stereotypes with families.

---

1 Consider the extent to which gender stereotypes may have had an effect on your own education. What influences can you identify from your family and what were the effects? To what extent have these affected your professional development?

---

2 How could any negative expectations have been addressed sensitively by your school and within your own family? What would you do now if a similar situation presented itself in your school?

---

3 How does this inform you about the principles for working with the families of pupils in your school over such issues?

---

4 What practices could you develop to help pupils and families in this area? How might the strategies and approaches vary for pupils from different year groups?

Before turning to the area of communicating with parents and families, it is important to address **the issue of care and control.** It seems that an unnatural splitting has occurred between these inter-related concepts and processes. This is another of the numerous negative outcomes of sex role stereotyping in families and in society. It generates a stereotypical view of men as 'controllers' and women as the 'carers' and produces an unnatural division of what are inherent and inter-related aspects of good parenting. Schools often mirror this distortion by splitting care and control functions. For example, when all the disciplinarian functions are allotted to the Head of Year and all the 'caring' to the school counsellor or form tutor. Or pastoral care systems are set up that focus solely on 'caring' or, alternatively, on controlling and punishing. Control is an important constituent of proper caring, but when exercised in isolation it can become brutish. Similarly, caring on its own can result in an over-emphasis on feelings. Each is part of the other, and when schools separate them they reduce them to useless caricatures which have no part in the life of the school.

The abuse of power and control in relationships can be very damaging. The most obvious, distressing and disturbing side of this occurs in the sexual abuse of children. Although this abuse involves sexual acts, it is not primarily about sexuality. It is more about an abuse of power.

Sexual relationships between men and women are frequently portrayed in stereotypical terms – men as active and initiating, women as passive. Men also usually have greater strength and size than women or children and are more able to insist by the use of the threat of physical force. 1 in 10 of all children by the time they reach of age of 16 has been sexually abused, usually by a man. This statistic is evenly spread across classes and backgrounds. Of these children 75% will have been abused by a male in their own family. The remaining 25% will have been abused by a male stranger. The incidence of women sexually abusing children is considered to be negligible. So, the sexual abuse of children is almost exclusively carried out by men in families on their own children (both girls and boys). Schools need to be aware of this when they suspect that a child may, through his or her behaviour, be expressing signs of sexual abuse. The usual principle of informing both parents/guardians over a child's behaviour in school will need to be thought through quite carefully, and may need modification. For example, if the school were to inform the male carer who was also the abuser, this could lead to more pressure on the child to keep the secret and, therefore, to continuing abuse. Schools need, through appropriate training, to be more aware of the incidence of abuse; the signs of abuse; the ways of monitoring children when abuse is suspected; the ways of promoting the sort of ethos in which children feel able to disclose when they are being abused; the gender issues in abuse and disclosure of abuse; and the policies and procedures to follow when it occurs. Action around child protection is one of the least palatable areas of the work of the pastoral team, but one which needs to be tackled, so that teachers feel some confidence about what and how they can help.

Communicating with families – what is the point and what are the issues?

The relationships that a school has with the parents and families of its pupils are important. When handled well, they are valued by schools and parents. Parents now have a legal right to know about the school, the curriculum offered to their child, and their child's progress. This area is no longer, therefore, a matter of choice for schools.

Schools may continue saying that the parents they really want to see never come to school and continue blaming parents for this state of affairs – this will produce no change. Alternatively, they can start to think more about the sorts of implicit and explicit messages that they convey to parents about how the school thinks about and values all families and how parents/guardians/significant family members are made to feel that they are valued as part of the education process and that they have an important role. Any school which takes this seriously will tend to find that developments and changes in its current practice are needed.

Before going any further we need to be clear about *why* we are working with parents. The legislation insists that we do, but is there any good reason other than that? And what will be our guiding principle for a home/school relations policy? A rationale for working with parents proposed by Atkin et al which is succinct as it is convincing is –

> **When parents understand what the school is trying to do, when they understand something of the role of educators, and when they take an active interest in, and provide support for their children's school work, then the effects can be both dramatic and long lasting.**[1]

This rationale could also provide us with the aims of our school-home programme which would be:

- **to communicate effectively to parents the aims of the school;**
- **to communicate effectively to parents the ways and means the school uses to achieve its aims – ie the curriculum in its broadest sense, which includes the school ethos, as well as the content and process of the curriculum;**
- **to communicate effectively to parents the importance of their active role in the education of their children.**

The basic issue we will be addressing in putting all of this into practice will, of course, be that of a practice which is sensitive to family arrangements and gender issues.

Within the home-school links policy some general principles and practices will need to be established. Some useful points in its formulation are:

- **to prioritise both communication and partnership with parents; to make it a policy that the school should be welcoming, positive and encouraging to parents; to work on ways of practically implementing this policy**
- **to make it a policy to show understanding and respect for all pupils and their families and for the various arrangements which constitute family life in the way schools represent families within the school, and to work on ways of practically implementing this policy**
- **to examine the home-school communication system so as to assess whether communications are sensitive to the realities and diversity of family life and to gender issues. This will involve scrutiny of the written and verbal forms of communication to ensure they are appropriate and effective and assessing the extent to which listening to parents is core to the process**

Atkin et al in their helpful book *Listening to Parents*[1] propose a method for **constructing a profile of home-school contacts**. This is done by using the following areas:

1 **Written communication**
2 **Spoken communication**
3 **Communication with individual parents**
4 **Communication with parents as a whole**

Activities which the school is currently involved in can be listed under these areas and a profile generated, such as the one overleaf (Figure 9.1).

When schools carry out this profiling exercise they will generate information which helps to review the range of opportunities they have currently for communication with parents. This process can help to identify areas of strength and weakness in the system that has been developed so far (and areas which need to be developed). Areas can then be examined and issues relating to gender sensitivity can be considered. In this way, schools may find, for example, that they rely mostly on written communication with parents and that spoken communication is not a well-developed area. This piece of information could lead to: consideration of a range of possible meetings; identification of a need for staff development sessions on verbal communication with parents in a range of different situations or on raising awareness about family arrangements; the development of a more appropriate checklists and record forms for use in entry interviews; etc.

Similarly, schools may find that, although all parents/guardians are invited to school for certain sorts of functions, they find that some attract more parents and others attract a disproportionate number of either men or women. Schools should endeavour to discover what the issues are for parents, and what parents find helpful and useful. The content and style of meetings will be critical, and so will access. The provision of a creche, for example, or the re-scheduling of meetings to offer more flexibility to working parents, may make a significant difference.

The range of activities in the home-school links programme is obviously crucial. The process of examining the range of activities is, therefore, an important one. This process can be helped by using the six major purposes of home-school links described by Atkin et al:[1]

1 **Informing parents eg about the curriculum, about events, about classroom life**
2 **Supporting parents and strengthening their expertise**
3 **Creating a dialogue with parents eg on children's progress**
4 **Involving parents in their own children's learning eg attending assemblies, home reading programmes**
5 **Involving parents in the life of the school eg parent helpers, fund raising**

Figure 9.1 From Atkin J. Bastiani; J. Goode J. (1988). *Listening to Parents* Croom Helm.

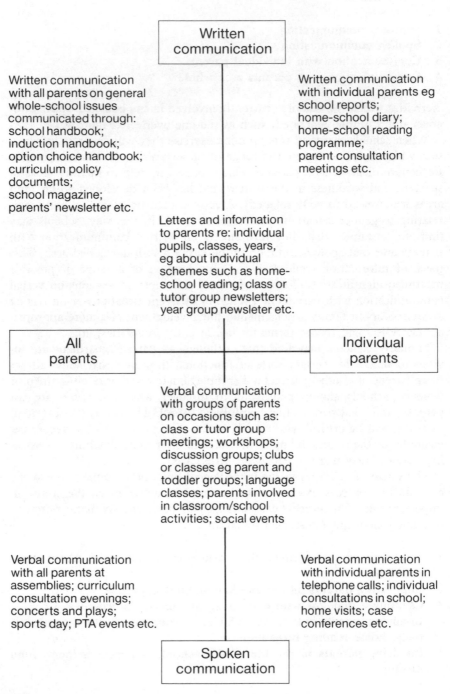

6 Listening to parents eg as providers of information and participants in decision making

Schools could use these six purposes as way of looking at their own home-school links to see which are well developed in terms of the range of activities for each purpose, and which less well developed. In each of the six areas a variety of school responses is possible and desirable. As part of this process it will be important to work out the extent to which the activities – whether they were arrangements for getting to know new families, curriculum evenings, or family meetings in school etc – are sensitive to equal opportunities issues. In order to find out what parents think of the communication systems the school is using they will need to be asked. A school survey of parents, using a random selection, should be possible. From the evidence we already have it seems likely that schools may be more satisfied than parents are with their home-school links programmes. For example, the National Consumer Council reporting in 1986 found that teachers are generally satisfied with their systems of communication with parents, whereas parents, apparently, would like more information than schools generally provide.[2] Maybe things have moved on since 1984? Each school will need to carefully review its own programme and find out what parents think about how the school communicates with them, what they would like to hear about and be involved in.

In summary parents want, and have a right to, advice and information and schools need to respond appropriately and communicate effectively. There can be little doubt that home-school links is an area which in most schools can be improved. We will now develop the ideas about the ways that schools can improve the ways they involve and inform parents into practical strategies.

Practical applications

> The aim of this activity is to examine the school's home links programmes. It can be carried out by the pastoral team for a particular year or house group, as a senior management team activity, or as one for a whole staff group. The individual reader can begin this process from her/his own experience.

> Take the four areas of a home-school programme:
> - written communication;
> - spoken communication;
> - communication with individual parents;
> - communication with parents as a whole
>
> use the foci of – a) all parents b) individual parents. What is your

school already doing in these areas? Generate your school profile of activities. Then, examine the profile and assess its balance in the four areas and two foci. Is it appropriately well balanced? If not, in which areas is it lacking? How could this unbalance be redressed?

Look at the six purposes: informing; supporting; creating a dialogue; involving in learning; involving in the life of the school; listening. Which of these are well developed in the school and which less well? How could the current range be strengthened and extended? What system exists to ensure regular review of the programme? How could it be carried out and by whom? How could parents be involved in that process? How does the school's management structure support the home-school links programme? How are staff at all levels supported in developing the necessary awareness of the issues in working with families, a programme of home-school links, the skills needed?

Communication with families – some practical considerations

When a school communicates with a pupil's family there are many considerations. The school will need to examine both written and verbal communication and make adaptations to ensure that stereotypical views are not inadvertently conveyed, and that communication is effective.

With written communication there will be a series of issues related to gender which will need to be considered. These will include to whom and how the communication is addressed and who will receive it, and the purposes, content and style of the communication. In other words, how accessible is it?

The first consideration is **to whom the communication is sent, who is likely to receive it and the titles and names which are used.** Most communications between school and home, be they some form of general information or newsheet to all the parents, personal letter, or whatever, are handed by children or young people to a woman. It seems that schools often anticipate this by putting the title Mrs on letters home. Sometimes pupils are encouraged to write titles on the envelope, and on these occasions form tutors or subject teachers often provide a model on the blackboard. The model provided is often 'Mr and Mrs' with the implication that the child will then simply add her or his surname. Clearly, neither of these practices is acceptable since neither shows due sensitivity to gender issues in relation to the use of titles, nor to child rearing arrangements. Variations on the title used by a parent could occur for the child who lives in a step-family; who is being reared by a single parent (of either sex); whose parents are unmarried; who lives with members of her or his extended family; who lives in care in a foster home, or a local authority children's home. On the other hand these forms of address could, equally, be entirely correct. So, if models are being provided in class a range should be presented. The use of personal and family names is another sensitive area. In some schools it has been known for teachers to change certain pupils' names, which they claim are difficult to spell or to pronounce, or which they simply prefer to change. This practice is one which undermines the pupil, it can also undermine her or his cultural heritage, and make the pupil feel singled out in a way that can be embarrassing and may provoke name calling by other pupils. Neither parents nor pupils should be demeaned by having their titles changed to fit stereotypical 'norms' about families, nor their names abbreviated or simplified to egocentric or ethnocentric substitutes.

Teachers often feel more comfortable with written than verbal communication with parents and this is major tool in the home-school links programme. Therefore, it is important for the school to closely scrutinise all their written communication. We have already looked at systematic ways of reviewing the areas and the range of activities in each area in relation to the purposes of communication. **The content, style and layout are elements which will need to be closely examined.**

With any written communication the content should be relevant to the purpose of the communication; content, presentation style and language are all inter-related aspects. One way of reviewing these is to collect all the communications sent out to parents over a set period of time and to look at them in terms of their purposes and how well those are achieved. A key question will be how accessible they are to the 'audience' of parents. These are the features which have a major effect on how the family views the school, and the extent to which it is seen as an approachable and friendly place or a formal and bureaucratic sort of place. A formal style of communication is not appropriate for most purposes of home-school communication. But an attractive and professional looking finish makes a communication more accessible. The content of any communication needs to be examined closely. There may be unintended messages which imply sexist, or racist, attitudes, for example, the use of illustrations, or elements of language use – such as the sole use of the pronoun 'he' when 'he' or 'she' is equally valid (a simple solution to this is to use 's/he'); or of activities which represent women and/or people from ethnic minority groups in negative or stereotypical roles. All of these are aspects of communication which should be considered by the school so as to ensure that its practice is in line with its equal opportunities policy.

A survey of the written communications sent out would help the school to examine the impressions of the school that are being conveyed to families. An assessment could then be made of the extent to which the balance might be towards one particular purpose rather than another. Taking the purposes of: informing, supporting, creating a dialogue, involving parents in their own child's learning, involving parents in the life of the school, listening to parents – it should be possible to make an assessment of the balance. So, for example, whereas information is obviously important, if it is all a family get from a school then how are they to feel engaged and involved in the process of education? If the school survey also looked at language, style, content and presentation, then a fuller picture could be built up of the impression given by the school through its written communication. Feedback could also be asked of parents about their views of the school's accessibility through its written communication, through small surveys in particular year groups. This would be an appropriate task for the pastoral team and in this way the school could work to improve the effectiveness of its communication.

Sometimes schools feel they have particular **difficulty in involving parents of particular pupils.** This can be interpreted by the school as lack of interest on the part of the adult carers. Undoubtedly some are less concerned and some are more reluctant to become involved, but we need to be careful about attributing motives and intentions to parents who do not apparently respond since often this can be due to a failure in communication. Sometimes it is the case that parents are not asked to come to school until there is a serious concern about a child's behaviour or progress. It is little wonder that this may prove problematic for a parent who does not feel confident and at ease in a school setting. Many teachers say they feel that way when they visit their own child's school – how much harder must it be for parents who feel unconfident about schools and teachers?

Communication over 'mundane' matters is, therefore, crucial, since these communications are often the major source of information about the school, and they are one means whereby parents and families build up a picture of the school. A school's written communication can usually be made more accessible through attention to content, layout, style and language, and by translating text into community languages.

Verbal communication with parents is another key area. The purposes of verbal communications with parents are similar to those of written ie informing, engaging, involving and listening. Verbal communication requires considerable interpersonal communication skills on the part of the teacher in terms of verbal and non-verbal behaviours which are appropriate to a range of situations. Teachers will need training in the skills needed and the requirements of different situations. **Communication may be with groups of parents or individual parents, at school or out of school.** For example, home visits, individual parent interviews, tutor group parents' evenings, discussion groups, workshops, telephone calls etc will all need consideration in a training programme. This training will be in communication skills which are sensitive to issues of gender and race.

One useful way to address the range of skills needed in a range of different meetings is to use the notion of **phases of the meeting.** These can provide a framework for analysing and practising the skills needed, and for reviewing the effectiveness of meetings. **A useful framework is one with the following five phases:**

1 *Pre-meeting*
   clarifying purposes
   planning the structure
   planning the process
   planning the setting for the meeting
2 *Beginning/social stage*
   welcoming
   engaging
   clarifying purposes
   clarifying expectations
3 *Middle*
   listening and prompting
   asking
   responding
   exploring and clarifying ideas and meanings
   sharing understandings
4 *Ending*
   summarising
   agreeing on outcomes and action
   agreeing on a form of record
   planning follow-up
   reviewing the meeting: eliciting feedback from the participants
5 *Post-meeting*
   reviewing the structure
   reviewing the process
   reviewing the purposes
   reviewing the outcomes
   initiating action
   monitoring
   planning the follow-up

This framework can be applied to home visits, to school-based interview etc and to verbal communication with individual parents and with groups of parents.

Different sorts of skills are needed for different types of meetings/ size of group/purpose. It is usually the case that most work is needed to develop the skills of effective verbal communication with individual parents. These skills can be developed and practised through simulations and role plays. The use of case studies is also particularly useful as a way of raising issues. Situations which the pastoral team and subject teachers are likely to encounter in their everyday practice can also be used to explore issues and develop skills in training sessions with the pastoral team (see the activity on developing communication skills – below).

When there is a need to communicate with a group of parents the teacher will need to be aware of the dynamics of groups which, of course, includes gender issues. In large groups there are clear tendencies for opinions to polarise, for few people to speak, for men to dominate, for men to ask significantly more questions than women, and for conflict to emerge more easily than in small groups. Added to this, teachers are often accustomed to talking to large groups (eg in year or school assemblies) and to seeing large groups as being homogeneous (eg a whole year group). If teachers are to communicate effectively with parents in large group situations then schools will need to be aware of these issues in large groups, and in their role in relation to large groups, and to work on the skills of engaging parents appropriately, so that they feel involved and do not feel intimidated, patronised, or left out.

Successful methods for addressing these issues in large groups of parents include:

- **the main speaker being a woman;**
- **input to the whole group kept to a minimum;**
- **the use of visual aids to help communicate purpose and main points succinctly;**
- **the use of small group discussion within the large group;**
- **the use of pairs ('talk to the person next to you'), before any questions are taken;**
- **breaking the large group down into smaller discussion groups;**
- **breaking the large group down into smaller discussion groups and using group facilitators for discussion.**

Large group effects, when the participants do not know each other, can occur in groups as small as ten, so teachers who work with smaller groups of parents will also need some training in the issues and skills of large group management and facilitation.

Verbal communication with individual parent(s) or guardian(s) raises another set of issues. These revolve around who is/are the main carer(s) for the child, how significant adults are engaged in the meeting, what is its purpose and how is it conducted. Gender issues are central to all of these.

Issues to do with titles and names which have already been discussed will also be relevant. Another issue which may arise is the pupil's use of the terms 'Mum' and 'Dad'. These should be acknowledged according to the usage in that particular family. For example, in the case of a child living with extended family members it may be that the child uses those terms to refer to an Aunt or Uncle. In a family in which there are step-children, it may be very important that a step-mother of father is *not* referred to as

Mum or Dad, or the opposite could equally be the case. Schools need to enquire about these things and not take them for granted.

The issue of power and how that is handled by the school is also crucial. That is to say, in any interview between school and home, there is potential for a power imbalance. This can occur when the school has asked the parent to visit over a particular issue, or when the school fails to recognise the unique knowledge, perspective and/or responsibility of the parent(s). It may also be exacerbated by the sex of the interviewer and interviewee – ie a male teacher interviewing female carer may set up a particular power dynamic. The interviewing style used can also have an effect and this is often influenced by the events leading up to the meeting. For example, teachers sometimes tend to use an over formal style when a pupil's behaviour has led to the meeting. The unintended result of this can be for the parent to feel blamed and to behave defensively, in a passive or an aggressive fashion. This is unlikely to lead to the real communication and joint problem solving which is needed on these occasions. Of course the school can offer parents opportunities for interviews/meetings/consultations outside crises, and the more this occurs as a part of 'normal' school life the more relaxed and equitable the relationships between teachers and parents are likely to be.

One area which often causes difficulties in communication is the assumption that in any household a woman is solely responsible for child rearing. This leads to invitations to women alone (in letters routinely addressed to Mrs X) to come for interviews. Clearly this is not a problem if a couple make a decision over who is able to attend a school meeting – but it is a problem if schools force choices in particular ways by whom they invite. A parent should be able to come to a meeting at school alone, with a partner, or with a friend. This should apply for married and unmarried couples and single parents and this should be made explicit.

Single parents of both sexes often feel particularly offended by the way they are treated by schools. They, and their children, are often led to feel that a single parent home is not as adequate as that of a home comprising two parents. There is no conclusive evidence to suggest that children brought up in single parent families suffer more as a result of single handed child rearing, and many children suffer significantly less (especially when there have been abusive relationships in the family). The crucial element, as in two parent families, is the quality of care offered by the carer. Single parents are clearly no less capable of caring for their children and are often more committed to it. Schools should, therefore, avoid asking questions or making statements in interviews which could be offensive to single parents – such as, 'How do you manage to cope on your own?' or, 'Wouldn't if be better if...'

In order to be effective communicators teachers need training in interviewing skills and in sensitivity to gender issues in interpersonal communication. Particular attention will need to be paid to communication styles. There is no one style that all men and women use, but research into interpersonal communication styles in mixed and same sex interactions suggests that there are observable differences in the verbal and non-verbal communication behaviours of men and women. The tendency in conversations between men and women is for men to determine and to lead the topic, to make more direct statements, to interrupt more and to use fewer verbal and non-verbal prompts. All of this leads them to dominate and control mixed sex conversations. In conversations with other men, however, more turn-taking is observed. Women, on the other hand, in conversations with both men and women tend to use a more tentative style of language, using so-called 'hedges' such as *you know, sort of, just.* Women are more likely to add to what the previous speaker has said (rather than changing the subject or offering a competing idea); to use verbal and non-verbal prompts which encourage the speaker to continue, such as the use of questions, of *mmh...mmhs*, head nodding, facial expression, smiling, eye contact, learning forward etc. All of these behaviours tend to support the other speaker continuing to speak.

Although this behaviour has been observed and reported as a gender issue, as with most gender issues it is essentially an issue of power – who chooses to exert power in interactions and in what manner. Of course there are individual differences and many women have learned to vary their communication style so as to make themselves heard in situations which would otherwise be difficult. Teachers need to be aware of these gender and power issues in communication and to have opportunities to review their own communication styles and to practise a repertoire of skills for effective communication.

Activities

1   Working with parents The aim of this activity is to develop sensitivity to the issues and to develop and practise communication skills.
Choose one of the following situations:

a)   a couple come to discuss option choices for their daughter
b)   an uncle comes to discuss the placement of an 11-year-old girl who he refers to as his daughter in the first year
c)   parents are requested to come to discuss the difficult behaviour of their XX year old (decide on the age)
d)   a parent wants to set up a parents' group on a particular theme
e)   the school is interviewing parents about what they would like in the home-school programme

Allocate the roles – then leave the parent(s) and the teacher(s) for a couple of minutes to work out some aspects of content of the role and the situation (beware of having too much content). Carry out the role play, then reflect on the process. Ask the people role playing the parents how the experience was for them. Did they feel they were heard and understood? What helped in that process? What did the teachers do that was particularly helpful? What could they have done differently? Then reflect on:

- the assumptions that were made on both sides about power. Who was seen as having the knowledge and expertise? How did that affect how people felt and how they behaved?
- the gender issues that were explicit or implicit in what happened in how the meeting was set up eg was an assumption made about the particular sex of parent and on what grounds? During the meeting what gender issues were in evidence?

Then try out the role play again and see how it can be improved on.

For role plays a) b) c) include the pupil in the role play. What issues were raised and how could they be addressed?

This activity can be used as a discussion, but it is important that at some stage teachers actually practice the skills and get constructive feedback on how they can improve their effectiveness in communicating.

2 Working with parents The aim of this activity is to develop effective communication skills for different phases of meetings.

Take one phase and work out what you might do to cover the main points. Exchange ideas with other colleagues and put together all the ideas that have been generated. Evaluate the ideas and then try them out. Ask one person to observe and to offer feedback from their perspective. What worked well? What situations would require modifications?

1 Pre-meeting
   clarifying purposes; planning the structure; planning
   the process; planning the setting for the meeting
2 Beginning/Social stage
   welcoming; engaging; clarifying purposes; clarifying
   expectations
3 Middle
   listening and prompting; asking; responding; exploring
   and clarifying ideas and meanings; sharing
   understandings
4 Ending
   summarising; agreeing on outcomes and
   action; agreeing on a form of record; planning
   follow-up; reviewing the meeting: eliciting feedback
   from the participants

5 Post-meeting
  reviewing the structure; reviewing the process;
  reviewing the purposes; reviewing the outcomes;
  initiating action;
  monitoring; planning the follow-up

In this chapter the focus has been on families and how schools can begin to work more effectively with families. In order to do this schools need to be sensitive to, value and welcome the diversity of families and family life. This can only be done if teachers learn about that diversity and the issues for schools in responding to it positively.

We are all products of families in which there are assumptions and expectations about gender roles. It is important, therefore, to examine the processes and beliefs in our own familial conditioning. In that way we can become more aware of the role of families in the production and perpetuation of gender roles. We will also be clearer about the fact that working with families around these issues requires a high level of sensitivity and skill. No doubt the reader of this chapter has already started that process of self reflection. The next stage will be to introduce the ideas and activities to colleagues in school so that the process is carried into and developed through the pastoral team.

A major aim of the chapter has been to argue that the home-school programme is an area which deserves and needs considerable thought, planning, and expertise. If it is to be an effective programme then gender issues will need to be addressed explicitly. For this to occur pastoral teams will need to prioritise working with parents and families and develop the skills to achieve their pastoral goals.

References

1 Atkin, J., Bastiani, J., Goode, J. (1988) *Listening to Parents*. Croom Helm.
2 Woods, (1984) *Parents and School*. Welsh Consumer Council and Schools Council Committee for Wales.

Further reading

Coates, J. (1986) *Women, Men and Language*. Longman.
Deegan, M. J., Hill, M. (eds) (1987) *Women and Symbolic Interaction*. Unwin Hyman.
Frieze, I., Parsons, J., Johnson, P., Rubli, O., Zellman, G. (1980) *Women and Sex Roles*. Norton and Co.

Gorell Barnes, G. (1984) *Working With Families*. Macmillan.

Johnson, D., Ransom, E. (1983) *Family and School*. Croom Helm.

Maher, P. (ed) (1987) *Child Abuse: The educational perspective*. Blackwell.

McRobbie, A. and Nava, M. (1984) *Gender and Generation*. Macmillan.

Peake, A. (1988) *Working with Sexually Abused Children: a resource pack for professionals*. The Children's Society.

Priestley, P. and McGuire, J. (1983) *Learning to Help – basic skills exercises*. Tavistock Publications.

Notes on the contributors

Sue Adler works in the Curriculum Resources Library of the London Institute of Education, having previously been the Gender librarian for the Learning Resources of Inner London Education Authority.

Sue Askew is a lecturer in Health Education in the Department of Curriculum Studies at the London Institute of Education. She has taught in London comprehensive schools and has been an advisory teacher for equal opportunities, and previously for Health, Social and Personal Education.

Lesley Kant is Deputy Director and Chief Inspector for the London Borough of Merton. She taught in London schools for ten years before moving into teacher training. Later she worked at the Schools Council as Principal Adviser in examinations and assessment work, where she was also responsible for the Council's equal opportunities programme. Prior to joining Merton in 1988, she was a member of the Norfolk LEA inspectorate and Country INSET Co-ordinator.

Caroline Lodge is Headteacher of George Orwell School, London. She taught History for nine years in Coventry, ran an education support unit in Warwickshire, has been Head of Year, Deputy Head (pastoral and curriculum). She is Chair of London Region NAPCE* and a member of the national executive.

---

* NAPCE is the National Association for Pastoral Care in Education. It is an active association with over 2000 members. The production of this book was in part stimulated by the production of the NAPCE document *The Pastoral Contribution to Gender Equity*, written in 1986 by a working group which included some of the present contributors.
For further details contact:
NAPCE, c/o University of Warwick, Coventry CV4 7AL tel 0203 523810

Colleen McLaughlin is Tutor in Personal and Social Education at Cambridge Institute of Education. She has been an advisory teacher for guidance and counselling, a Head of Year, an English teacher and a trained school counsellor. She is presently involved in thinking about and running effective in-service courses on gender issues.

Carol Ross is presently the Equal Opportunities Coordinator for Islington schools and also teaches at the London Institute of Education. For the past seven years she has been involved in equal opportunities and curriculum development, pastoral work, producing materials and advisory work.

Gill Venn is head of the language and communication faculty at Kelmscott School in Waltham Forest. She has taught in both mixed and single-sex schools. The research conducted for her Masters degree was concerned with the pastoral curriculum.

Patsy Wagner is Deputy Principal Educational Psychologist in the London Borough of Kensington and Chelsea, having been a teacher and Head of Department of Compensatory Education in London comprehensive school. She is also a trained family therapist and a committee member of London region NAPCE.

Jennifer Walden is a teacher of English at Tom Hood School in Waltham Forest. She has also taught in Higher Education and has been a member of the Behavioural Support Team with a Schools Psychological Service in London. She was recently seconded for one term by Waltham Forest, in association with the London Institute of Education to produce a report for her LEA on gender issues in classrooms.

Chris Watkins is course tutor to the Diploma in Pastoral Care and has also been Senior Tutor (INSET) at the London Institute of Education. Work on gender has included collaboratively writing packs for teachers, running conferences, workshops and men's groups. He is vice-chair of NAPCE.

Index

190

pressure groups 25
PSE 2
PSE courses 83, 84, 120–135
psychiatric illness 170
punishment 1, 23
pupil material 102–108
pupil-pupil interaction 56, 68–72
pupils' expectations 152
'putting down' 68

quotas 34

racial harassment 51
racism 47, 51
range of significant adults 163
Records of Achievement 118
recruitment 19, 27, 33, 39
relationship breakdowns 163
role models 19
role play 110–11
'roles in the home' 123–4
romantic goals 87, 90

scapegoating 88, 90
school climate 2, 80
school governors 35
school guidelines 38
school policy 111, 113
Section 28, 150
selection procedures 40
self as a learner 93
self in the organisation 93
self-image 87
separation of boys and girls 70–2
separations 163
sex differentiation 143
sex discrimination 33, 34
Sex Discrimination Act (1975) 33, 34
sex education 149–51
sex stereotyping 37, 47
sexism 7, 37, 46, 51, 128, 167
sexual abuse of children 172–3
sexual harassment 148, 153
sexual self 93, 148, 151
shared responsibility for child rearing
    163

single-handed parenting 162–3, 183
single-parent households 161
single-sex groupings 71
small group activities 96, 98, 115
social education programmes 90
social inequality 47–8
social learning 98
social self 93, 148, 151
space 21, 29–30, 56–7
spoken (verbal) communication 175,
    177, 178, 179, 182
staff development 20
staff issues 19
status 19, 27
step-children 182
step-families 161, 164–5
stereotypes 9, 10, 124
stereotypical behaviours 156
stereotyping 14, 17, 23, 167
stimulus materials 99
structured discussion 88, 100

talk 63–64
teacher appraisal 152
teacher-pupil interaction 56, 64–8, 156
teacher-teacher interactions 156–7
time 56, 60–2
titles and names 178
training and development 20, 40
transfer of learning 100
tutor 18, 20, 94, 98
tutor group 88
tutorial programmes 84, 94
TVEI 46, 153

vocational choice 153
vocational guidance 145, 153–4
vocational self 93

wall displays 22
whole group discussion 115
whole-school processes 2
working parties 38
written communication 175, 177, 178